D0758657

The Wainwright Memorial Walk

'This tour is a most comprehensive one. Limited as we are by time, it is impossible to visit every corner of Lakeland, yet this programme, if followed conscientiously, will lead us everywhere worth mentioning.

It will be ARDUOUS, but the reward will be well worth the work. It will avoid the tourists, the roads, the picnic-spots.

It is the claim of this programme that EVERY lake, EVERY valley, EVERY mountain, will be seen if not actually visited.'

A. WAINWRIGHT, 1931

The Wainwright Memorial Walk

A. Wainwright

FRANCES LINCOLN

Frances Lincoln Limited
4 Torriano Mews
Torriano Avenue
London NW5 2RZ
www.franceslincoln.com

Originally published by Michael Joseph 1993 (under the title
Wainwright's Tour in the Lake District) and 1998
First published by Frances Lincoln 2004

Printed and bound in Thailand

A CIP catalogue record is available for this book
from the British Library

ISBN 978 0 7112 2402 5

Some of the material appearing in this book is taken
from works previously published by the Westmorland Gazette, Kendal

9 8 7 6 5 4 3 2

Contents

Sources and Acknowledgements

The text for this book has been taken, wherever possible, from the writings of A. Wainwright. The main route directions are set in *italic*. Copy set in **bold** has been added by the publisher to give up-to-date information; however, where the linking copy is very short, the text remains in roman type to ease the flow of reading. Very occasionally, words or phrases have been slightly altered from AW's original, again to form a more satisfactory link, and these too remain in roman. Betty Wainwright, AW's widow, has seen and approved these changes.

Text and maps have been taken from the following books, and the date of first publication is set beside each title.

The titles listed below are all copyright © Michael Joseph 1992

THE PICTORIAL GUIDES TO THE LAKELAND FELLS
Book One: The Eastern Fells 1955
Book Two: The Far Eastern Fells 1957
Book Three: The Central Fells 1959
Book Four: The Southern Fells 1960
Book Five: The Northern Fells 1962
Book Six: The North Western Fells 1964
Book Seven: The Western Fells 1966

A COAST TO COAST WALK 1973
THE OUTLYING FELLS OF LAKELAND 1974

FELLWANDERER: *The Story behind the Guidebooks* 1966
WESTMORLAND HERITAGE 1974
THREE WESTMORLAND RIVERS 1979
A LAKELAND SKETCHBOOK 1969
A SECOND LAKELAND SKETCHBOOK 1970
A THIRD LAKELAND SKETCHBOOK 1971
A FOURTH LAKELAND SKETCHBOOK 1972
A FIFTH LAKELAND SKETCHBOOK 1973
LAKELAND MOUNTAIN DRAWINGS
   Volume One 1980
   Volume Two 1981
   Volume Three 1982
   Volume Four 1983
   Volume Five 1984
OLD ROADS OF EASTERN LAKELAND 1985
EX-FELLWANDERER 1987
FELLWALKING WITH A CAMERA 1988

*The titles listed below are all copyright © The Estate of the late
A. Wainwright and the copyright date is as the date of publication set beside each title*

FELLWALKING WITH WAINWRIGHT 1984
WAINWRIGHT'S COAST TO COAST WALK 1987
WAINWRIGHT ON THE LAKELAND MOUNTAIN
   PASSES 1989
WAINWRIGHT'S FAVOURITE LAKELAND
   MOUNTAINS 1991
WAINWRIGHT IN THE VALLEYS OF LAKELAND 1992

The six-day walk planned by A. Wainwright, and published as the illustrated *Wainwright's Tour in the Lake District* in 1993, has been re-shaped into eleven stages, each with more realistic mileages than the punishing target set by AW. The days which have been split now have new beginnings and/or ends, and copy has been inserted to describe these. The eleven-stage walk may be completed in a single period, in several sections, or as individual day walks. A car would be necessary at the end of most of the stages in the last two alternatives, although there are three stages which describe a circuit. There have been a few additional amendments made in this edition, to reflect some of the problems of erosion which occur on parts of the walk; Eric Robson and his researcher colleague David Powell-Thompson must be thanked for supplying details of these changes.

In the first edition, the pages of the original copy of AW's plan for the walk were reproduced, courtesy of Hazel Maudsley, widow of W. E. Maudsley, one of AW's companions on the walk. For this edition, an amended typeset version of AW's list is included. The spellings and names in use today are followed – for example Scarth Gap not Scarf Gap.

Almost all the maps have been taken from Wainwright's Pictorial Guides to the Lakeland Fells; however, Chris Jesty – the cartographer entrusted by AW to produce maps for some of the books written when his own eyes were not sharp enough for detailed work – has contributed an extension to the first route map linking Orrest Head to Sour Howes 2, and a new map for the end of Day Three, linking Clough Head 4 to the hamlet of Scales. He has also drawn the map on pages xiv–xv which shows the entire route.

Chris Jesty walked the entire route to check that the major details given in the text still hold true today, and the book would have been the poorer without his vigilance and eye for detail. The maps were only revised where necessary to enable the route to be followed easily. These small amendments, as with the changes to the text, have all been approved by Betty Wainwright.

JENNY DEREHAM
Editor of the Wainwright Walking Books

SIGN REFERENCES
(signs used in the maps and diagrams)

Good footpath
(sufficiently distinct to be followed in mist)

Intermittent footpath
(difficult to follow in mist)

Route recommended but no path
(if recommended one way only, arrow indicates direction)

Wall   Broken wall

Fence   Broken fence

Marshy ground   Trees

Crags   Boulders

Stream or River
(arrow indicates direction of flow)

Waterfall   Bridge

Buildings   Unenclosed road

Contours (at 100' intervals)   1900 1800 1700

Summit-cairn ▲   Other (prominent) cairns △

Introduction to original edition
by W. E. Maudsley

I worked with Alf in Blackburn Town Hall and was sitting opposite him at the large office desk at the time he drew up his 1931 'Grand Tour' of Lakeland.

Alf took his first holiday in the Lakes in 1930 when he was twenty-three. Leaving his day-to-day life in the claustrophobic environment of the close-packed terrace houses of a Lancashire mill town, he found himself in a world of unbelievable beauty. That was the week which changed his life. On his return, he made plans to revisit the area, and with the care and attention to detail that was typical of him, he drew up his first guide to walking in the Lake District, a walk to be made with three colleagues from the Borough Treasurer's office in Blackburn: myself, Jim Sharples and Harry Driver.

The first day of the holiday was perhaps ill-fated. We had to travel from Blackburn to Windermere by bus and then do a sixteen-mile walk over the hills. Arriving in Windermere after midday, we found the hills grey with clouds. We set out to climb High Street, and it was not long before it started to rain. We were approaching Ill Bell and Froswick when the rain became very heavy and as it was by now early evening we decided the first day's programme could not be completed. We descended to the

Troutbeck area and found accommodation for the night.

Although we did not complete the whole programme as AW planned it, we followed it for most of the way. I remember we had to leave out climbing Blencathra, Grasmoor and Pillar. Looking at it with hindsight, the programme was a strenuous challenge as we were a young and inexperienced group. I was twenty and on my first visit to the Lakes, and Alf was twenty-four with just his first exploratory visit the year before.

In 1991, my memories of that Lakeland walk with Alf Wainwright in 1931 are dim with the dust of six decades. The fellwalkers of today can perhaps achieve Alf's first written concept of his Lakeland objectives and commitment in its entirety.

ERIC MAUDSLEY, August 1991

Introduction to this edition
by Eric Robson

I first met Alfred Wainwright shortly after I came to live in the Lake District. His reputation went before him. He would be difficult, monosyllabic, even cantankerous. Nervously I sat down across the table from the great man in a less than splendid caff in Kendal to which I'd been summoned to have ham and chips and to be given the once over. He pinched a slice of ham from my plate to take home for Tottie the cat. I pretended not to notice, he beamed and all was well with the world. It was the start of five years of some of the happiest filming I've ever been part of.

The BBC series we made together proved him to be very different from the dour old codger of Lakeland folklore. He was kind and erudite, philosophical and passionate. I only knew him as an old man with slightly dodgy legs and failing eyesight. But if you want to meet this greatest of Lakeland explorers at the height of his powers then follow the Memorial Walk.

He devised it in 1930 with the maps spread out on his bedroom floor in Blackburn. It was to be an adventure for some of his pals in the Borough Treasurer's office: a six-day walk which they attempted during the Whitsun holiday in 1931. It's an adventure still but rather more manageable now since its 104 miles and thirty-five thousand feet of ascent have been split into eleven day stages

We filmed the Memorial Walk in the glorious summer and early autumn of 1997 as part of a video tribute to AW. It's a walk that does everything it promises. In a quite remarkable way it captures the spirit of Lakeland and the geographic and poetic relationships between the summits that crowd this most intimate upland paradise.

On my journey through the mountains, made long after AW had gone back to the gritty summit of Haystacks for the last time, I discovered another Alfred Wainwright – young, enthusiastic, bursting with humour, rash and forever curious about this landscape and the people who moulded it. All these years on he's still a great walking companion.

ERIC ROBSON, January 1998

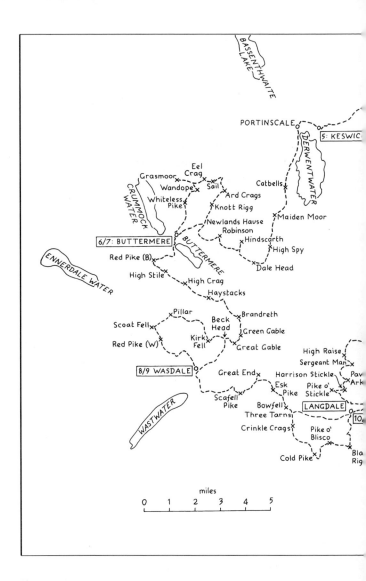

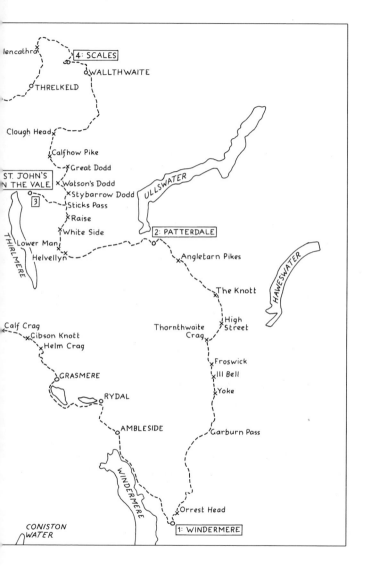

lencathra

4: SCALES

WALLTHWAITE

THRELKELD

Clough Head

Calfhow Pike

Great Dodd

ST. JOHN'S
N THE VALE

Watson's Dodd

Stybarrow Dodd

3

Sticks Pass

Raise

White Side

Lower Man

Helvellyn

THIRLMERE

ULLSWATER

2: PATTERDALE

Angletarn Pikes

HAWESWATER

The Knott

Calf Crag

Gibson Knott

Helm Crag

Thornthwaite
Crag

High
Street

Froswick

Ill Bell

GRASMERE

Yoke

RYDAL

AMBLESIDE

Garburn Pass

WINDERMERE

CONISTON
WATER

Orrest Head

1: WINDERMERE

Why *does* a man climb mountains? Why has he forced his tired and sweating body up here when he might instead have been sitting at his ease in a deckchair at the seaside. On the face of it, the thing doesn't make sense.

Yet more and more people are turning to the hills; they find something in these wild places that can be found nowhere else. It may be solace for some, satisfaction for others: the joy of exercising muscles that modern ways of living have cramped, perhaps; or a balm for jangled nerves in the solitude and silence of the peaks; or escape from the clamour and tumult of everyday existence. It may have something to do with a man's subconscious search for beauty, growing keener as so much in the world grows uglier. It may be a need to re-adjust his sights, to get out of his own narrow groove and climb above it to see wider horizons and truer perspectives. Or it may be, and for most walkers it *will* be, quite simply, a deep love of the hills, a love that has grown over the years, whatever motive first took him there: a feeling that these hills are friends, tried and trusted friends, always there when needed.

It is question every man must answer for himself

From Book 4, Scafell Pike 24

Windermere to Patterdale

Orrest Head was the fell A. Wainwright climbed on the first day of his first visit to Lakeland in 1930; at the age of twenty-three, he had come here with a cousin for a holiday – his first holiday.

Beyond Preston we left the huge factories and mill chimneys behind and passed through a green and fertile landscape for many miles to Lancaster and beyond Lancaster the landscape was undulating and more varied. At one point of the journey I got my first ever glimpse of the sea in Morecambe Bay, and rising above its far horizon was a hazy background of lofty hills: a thrilling sight. The Lake District.

The bus took us through the long main street of Kendal and entered a colourful fairyland, the hills now bordering the road with occasional vistas of mountains, real mountains, and on topping a rise a long serpentine sheet of water fringed by glorious woodlands came into sudden view. Windermere!

Alighting from the bus, our first objective was Orrest Head, a recommended viewpoint nearby. Our way led up a lane amongst lovely trees, passing large houses that seemed to me like castles, with gardens fragrant with flowers. I thought how wonderful it must be to live in a house with a garden. The sun was shining, the birds singing. We went on, climbing steadily under a canopy of foliage, the path becoming rougher, and then, quite suddenly, we emerged from the shadows of the trees and were on a bare headland and, as though a curtain had dramatically been torn aside, beheld a magnificent view. It was a moment of magic, a revelation so unexpected that I stood transfixed, unable to believe my eyes.

I saw mountain ranges, one after another, the nearer starkly etched, those beyond fading into the blue distance. Rich woodlands, emerald pastures and the shimmering waters of the lake below added to a pageant of loveliness, a glorious panorama that held me enthralled. I had seen landscapes of rural beauty pictured in the local art gallery, but here was no painted canvas; this was real. This was truth. God was in his heaven that day and I a humble worshipper.

The mountains compelled my attention most. They were all nameless strangers to me, although I recognised the Langdale Pikes from photographs I had seen. They looked exciting and friendly. I fancied they were beckoning me to their midst. Cloud shadows chased across them as I watched, and momentarily they appeared gloomy and frightening, but with the return of the sun they were smiling again. Come on and join us, they seemed to say.

There were no big factories and tall chimneys and crowded tenements to disfigure a scene of supreme beauty, and there was a profound stillness and tranquillity. There was no sound other than the singing of larks overhead. No other visitors came.

*

At Whitsuntide the following year, AW chose Windermere and Orrest Head as the start of the walking tour he planned to undertake with three companions from the Borough Treasurer's office in Blackburn. He claimed that every lake, every valley and every mountain in Lakeland would be seen, if not visited, during the walk.

The way to Orrest Head is announced by a large signboard which proclaims its unrivalled views and states that it is a twenty minutes' walk to the top. It is the leftmost of three drives that leave the main road near the bus stops opposite the railway station, and is a tarmac strip initially. Almost at once a footpath goes off to the left: ignore this, keeping ahead and climbing gradually in a series of loops and bends. When a farm is reached

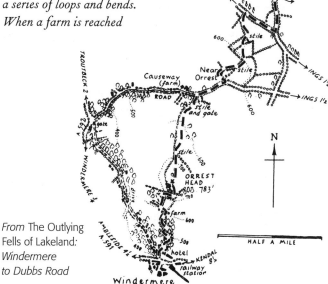

continued page 5

From The Outlying Fells of Lakeland: *Windermere to Dubbs Road*

the path becomes rough; further, it divides into three branches: take the one on the right by a wall to reach and enter a fenced lane with many seats. This leads to a kissing gate; in the wall alongside is a memorial tablet to Arthur Henry Heywood, whose family gave Orrest Head for public enjoyment. Through the gate and clear of trees at last, the view indicator on the summit of Orrest Head (783 feet) is seen on the right and soon reached.

AW did not leave written instructions in any of his books nor a map about the route between Orrest Head and Dubbs Reservoir but the extended map on the previous page and the following brief instructions will give guidance.

Leave the rocky top by a path heading north towards the white farmhouse of Causeway Farm. The path emerges onto a quiet by-road just to the right of the farm. Turn right into the lane but leave it shortly at Near Orrest. Here the path is difficult to find: turn left in the farmyard and go round the back of the farm buildings onto a footpath which leads north to the lane called Moorhowe Road on the Ordnance Survey map. Turn right and shortly afterwards, at Moor Howe, take the track called Dubbs Road which leads to Dubbs Reservoir.

Continue up Dubbs Road until it merges with Garburn Road.

There is little doubt that in late medieval times before the present lines of communication were established, a primitive road cut across the fells in the south-east corner of the Lake District between Windermere and Shap. The initial section of this ancient highway took advantage of a dip in the high skyline of the Ill Bell range to cross from Troutbeck to Kentmere, the depression being known as Garburn

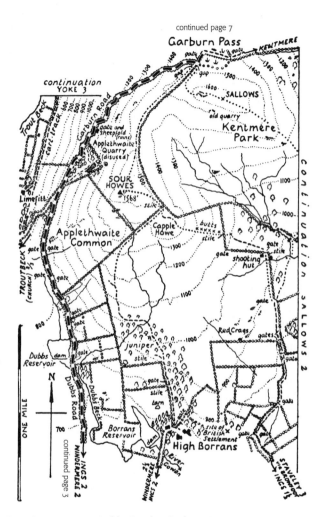

continued page 7

From Sour Howes 2: Dubbs Road to Garburn Pass

Pass, and Ordnance Survey maps still name the long lane leading to it as Garburn Road. Today, reduced in status to a bridleway, it is a route only for walkers, pony trekkers and motorbike scramblers.

The lane soon reaches the disused Applethwaite Quarry. Most old quarries are gloomy and repelling, with an air of desolation, but this one, masked by trees, is worthy of inspection since it retains relics of abandoned industry. This apart, there is little to relieve the tedium of the steady climb except for an excellent view of the Troutbeck valley, improving with every step.

On reaching the summit of Garburn Pass the route turns sharp left along a rising moorland, marshy in places, and narrowing as height is gained. The first summit reached is **YOKE**, *with a cairn at 2309 feet.*

Yoke is best known as the southern outpost of the Ill Bell ridge leading up to High Street from Garburn Pass, and is usually dismissed as a dull, unattractive mound. As seen from Troutbeck, this seems quite an accurate assessment, but the Kentmere flank is very different, abounding in much of interest. There is a good viewpoint, more particularly for the wide sweep of country and sea southwards. Of the Lakeland scene, the prospect due west is exceptionally attractive.

On the east/Kentmere flank, below the summit, is the formidable thousand-foot precipice of Rainsborrow Crag (the safety of which is a subject of disagreement between rock-climbers and foxes). A place of rocky excrescences, craggy tors and tumbled boulders, and a fine playground for the mountaineering novice. The presence of this fearful

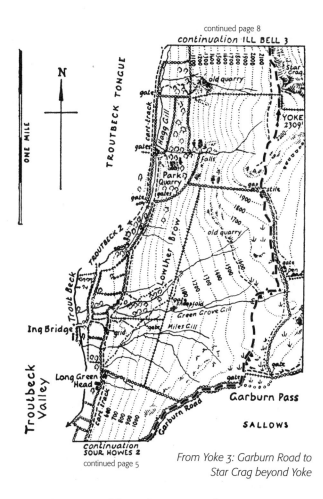

continued page 8

From Yoke 3: Garburn Road to Star Crag beyond Yoke

continued page 5

crag is not suspected from the summit of Yoke and attention is mainly focused on Ill Bell further along the ridge.

The graceful cone of Ill Bell is a familiar object to most

7

residents of south Westmorland and those visitors who approach Lakeland by way of Kendal and Windermere, although few who know it by sight can give it a name and fewer still its correct name. It is the dominating height on a steep-sided ridge, running north to High Street, and forms a most effective and imposing barrier between the Troutbeck and upper Kentmere valleys. It is linked by easy slopes to its neighbours, Yoke and Froswick, but both flanks are excessively steep. Ill Bell is distinctive and of good appearance, its peaked shape making it easily identifiable. The ridge on which it stands is probably the most popular fellwalk east of Kirkstone.

The walker who toils up to the top of Ill Bell may be pardoned for feeling that he has achieved a major climb that has played a part of some consequence in mountaineering

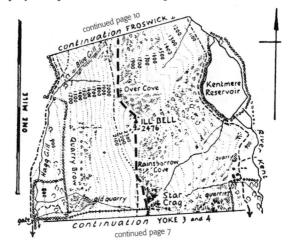

continued page 10

From Ill Bell 3: Star Crag to Ill Bell and Over Cove

history, for he finds himself confronted by an imposing array of cairns that would do credit to a Matterhorn. And in fact this is a real mountain top, small in extent and very rough.

Many of the cairns on the fells were erected by shepherds as identifiable landmarks in mist but most of those on the highest points of the summits can be attributed to walkers exuberant at their success on reaching the objective of their climb; summit cairns are always greeted with satisfaction after the effort of attaining them and many walkers perform the ritual of adding a stone.

*In fact, the summit of **ILL BELL**, at 2476 feet, can be bypassed along a level track across the western front, but it is unusually distinguished by having several mature cairns and a rash of infants, and commands such fine views that it should certainly be visited.*

This multiplicity of cairns, three of long-standing, augmented by others that have sprouted in recent years, crowd the top. It is a splendidly airy perch, and with the ground falling away out of sight all round, gives the impression of an island in the sky. Its special joy is a superb full-length view of Windermere.

*Turn left by the most northerly cairn on the summit of Ill Bell and find a path going down north-west to the next depression, beyond which is an easy climb on grass. Sheltering in the shadow of Ill Bell on High Street's south ridge is the lesser height of **FROSWICK**, 2359 feet.*

It takes its pattern from Ill Bell in a remarkable degree, almost humorously seeming to ape its bigger neighbour. Both flanks are very steep, the Kentmere side especially being a rough tumble of scree: there are crags here facing up the valley. The grassy Troutbeck slope, west, is notable for Froswick's one touch of originality, for it is cleft by a tremendous scree gully, Blue Gill, that splits the fellside from top to bottom.

Froswick's peaked appearance from afar holds out the promise of a small pointed summit. Small it is, and neat,

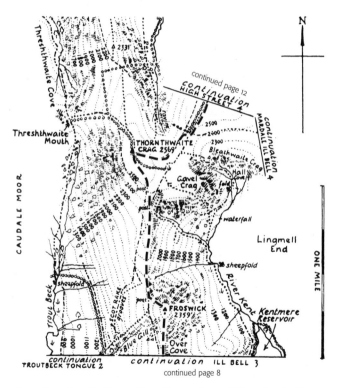

continued page 12
continued page 8

From Thornthwaite Crag 3: Over Cove to beyond Thornthwaite Crag

with a tidy cairn but it will hardly satisfy the seeker of spires.

It is an easy walk from the summit of Froswick to **THORN- THWAITE CRAG**. *The Crag can be identified from long distances, even from Kendal twelve miles away, by its handsome fourteen-foot obelisk of stone, a monument to the unknown craftsman who built it.*

Occupying a commanding position overlooking four valleys, Thornthwaite Crag (2569 feet) is one of the better-known fells east of Kirkstone, owing not a little of its fame to its tall pillar of stones, a landmark for miles around. Its name derives from the long shattered cliff facing west above the upper Troutbeck valley; there are also crags fringing the head of Hayeswater Gill and above the early meanderings of the River Kent. Apart from these roughnesses, the fell is grassy, the ground to the east of the summit forming a wide plateau before rising gently to the parent height of High Street, of which Thornthwaite Crag is a subsidiary; it has, however, a ridge in its own right, this being a narrow steep-sided shoulder that ends in Gray Crag, northwards. Streams flow in three directions: north to Ullswater, south to Windermere and south-east along the Kentmere valley.

It is sometimes difficult to recall the details of familiar summits but surely all who have climbed Thornthwaite Crag will identify it in memory by its remarkable column, one of the most distinctive cairns in Lakeland. It stands in the angle of a wall that traverses the summit. A few outcrops of flaky rock in the vicinity relieve the general grassiness of the top of the fell.

The tall column, the wall and adjacent high ground northwards between them interrupt the panorama and several 'stations' must be visited to see all there is to see. The view is good, but not amongst the best; the northern prospect, in particular, is best surveyed from the slope going down to Threshthwaite Mouth. The best feature in the scene is Windermere, to which the Troutbeck valley leads the eye with excellent effect.

Leave the beacon by a new path which leads to the summit of **HIGH STREET**. *A magnificent view of the Kentmere valley is seen from Gavel Crag.*

High Street is in stature the most massive of the fells on the far east of Lakeland, in altitude

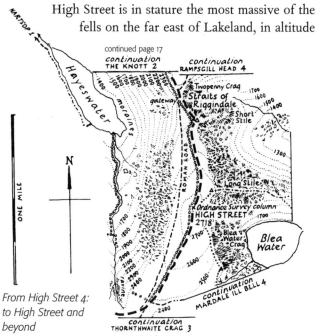

From High Street 4: to High Street and beyond

exceeding all the others in that company, and in strategic importance is the most influential, the summit being the apex of the longest ridge in the district and the central and culminating point of a complex pattern of valleys. Yet despite these credentials, High Street is unassuming and unpretentious and so accommodating to travellers that the Roman surveyors and engineers, during their early invasions of this country, laid a road across its broad top for the movement of troops and supplies in preference to their usual practice of seeking routes through the mountain passes. This ancient highway, still to be seen, gave High Street its unusual name.

The road constructed by the Romans to link their forts at *Galava* (Ambleside) and *Brocavum* (Brougham) during their military occupation of the country in the early centuries AD was the highest and most spectacular of the routes they adopted for the passage of troops and supplies. For twelve continuous miles, it maintains a height in excess of 2000 feet, following the crest of a lofty ridge in a wild landscape without refuge or shelter, and reaches 2718 feet. This made it the highest road in the country, a distinction held for eighteen centuries until modern engineers built a motor road to the top of Great Dunn Fell in the Pennines.

The Roman surveyors sent to reconnoitre a route found that High Street stood on the direct line between the two forts and must have been greatly relieved to find it relatively easy of access and that it presented no insuperable obstacles. The road is a monument to those surveyors and to the skill of the engineers who gave it a firm foundation in mossy and peaty ground, and testimony to the endurance of the legions of soldiers who, often in mist and cloud, tramped this long day's march of twenty-seven Roman miles (twenty-five English).

At each extremity, the actual line of the Roman road is a matter of conjecture, all traces being obscured by later building and farming development, but on the high ground of the central part, the route remains clearly defined, offering to non-Roman walkers the compelling challenge of a splendid high-level marathon.

Most of the high places in Lakeland have no mention in history books and, until comparatively recent times, when enlightened men were inspired to climb upon them for pleasure and exercise, it was fashionable to regard them as objects of awe and terror, and their summits were rarely visited. Not so High Street, which has been known and trodden, down through the ages, by a miscellany of travellers on an odd variety of missions: by marching soldiers, marauding brigands, carousing shepherds, officials of the Government, and now by modern hikers. Its summit has been in turn a highway and a sports arena and a race-course.

The long whale-backed crest of High Street attains a greater altitude than any other fell east of Kirkstone. Walking is easy on the grassy top: a factor that must have influenced the Roman surveyors to throw their road along it. But High Street is much more than an elevated and featureless field, for its eastern flank, which falls precipitously from the flat top to enclose the splendid tarn of Blea Water in craggy arms, is a striking study in grandeur and wildness; on this side a straight narrow ridge running down to

Mardale is particularly fine. The western face drops roughly to Hayeswater. To north and south, high ground continues to subsidiary fells along the main ridge.

The River Kent has its birth in marshes on the south slope but most of the water draining from the fells flows northwards to Haweswater and Hayeswater.

The top of High Street forms a gentle curve a mile in length between the Kentmere edge and the Straits of Riggindale and, completely covered in grass, serves as a large pasture for sheep and a soft carpet for other fellwalkers. It totally lacks features of natural interest, the only furniture being a crumbled stone wall along the ridge from one end to the other and a column of the Ordnance Survey. This column, like all such others, has become an antiquity, a thing of the past. No longer do the surveyors come on foot to make their triangulation readings from these columns. Photographs from aeroplanes and modern equipment give them the information they require with meticulous accuracy. A pity. These hoary columns were landmarks and old friends.

Although lacking in natural features of interest and having nothing to explore, the summit of High Street offers a splendid opportunity for rest, relaxation and quiet and undisturbed meditation: all is peaceful, and if the larks are singing overhead it is a blessed experience to be up here above the world and its worries. If visibility is clear there is a wonderful panorama westwards where the mountains of Lakeland are seen arrayed in a tumult of peaks on the distant horizon.

High Street's superior elevation over neighbouring fells is emphasised by the comprehensive views from the summit, the distant prospect between south-west and north, although partly obstructed by the Helvellyn range, being particularly good. The Coniston fells, the Scafells, Great Gable and Pillar appear with many other familiar heights on the horizon. Skiddaw and Blencathra are seen to the north, and there is a glimpse of Windermere to the south with Morecambe Bay beyond. But there is no depth to the views because of the flat top around the Ordnance column: the valleys are hidden and it is necessary to walk around the summit to reveal the more immediate surroundings. Those who can see no beauty in a wilderness should go and stand on the rim of Blea Water Crag.

From the summit of High Street, follow the edge of the escarpment north

On your right, you will pass Long Stile, a steep rocky spur of intimidating aspect. The pronounced dip in the ridge ahead is the narrow Straits of Riggindale and here a sudden stunning view of Mardale is revealed of the abyss of Riggindale – one of the highlights of the day's walk. It is in this area that sightings of Lakeland's resident golden eagles are most likely to occur.

Just past the Straits of Riggindale, the Roman road forks right for Rampsgill Head with the steep face of rock called Twopenny Crag falling into Riggindale. The route takes the left path.

The steep western slope descending from Rampsgill Head is arrested below the summit, just as the fall is gathering impetus, by a protuberance that takes the shape of a small conical hill. This is **THE KNOTT** *(2423 feet).*

The fell is a key point for walkers in this area, and

continued page 18

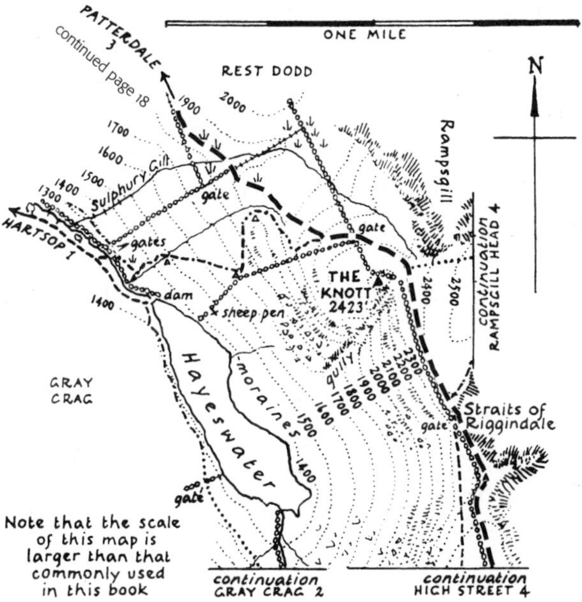
ONE MILE
PATTERDALE 3
REST DODD
N
Rampsgill
Sulphury Gill
gate
gates
dam
sheep pen
THE KNOTT 2423'
continuation RAMPSGILL HEAD 4
GRAY CRAG
Hayeswater
moraines
gully
Straits of Riggindale
gate
HARTSOP 1
Note that the scale of this map is larger than that commonly used in this book
continuation GRAY CRAG 2
continuation HIGH STREET 4

continued page 12

From The Knott 2: to beyond The Knott

although its short side rises barely a hundred feet from the main fell, its appearance is imposing when seen from other directions and especially from the Hartsop valley. Fans of scree litter its western flank which goes down steeply to Hayeswater; a tremendous scree gully here is The Knott's one interesting feature.

From The Knott, follow the path north-west to Satura Crag.

This is a fell of little interest and stands at an angle on the undulating grassy ridge coming down from the main watershed to the shores of Ullswater; its south-west slope drains into Hayeswater Gill. From the cairn on Satura Crag (only 25 yards from the path) there is a splendid view of Bannerdale, a view often missed by walkers.

The path now reaches Angle Tarn in a green hollow just below the summit of Angletarn Pikes, the next objective. Its indented shore and islets are features unusual in mountain tarns and it has for long, and deservedly, been a special attraction.

The charms of Angle Tarn, at all seasons of the year, are manifold: in scenic values, it ranks amongst the best of Lakeland tarns.

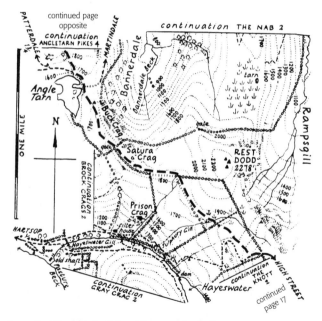

From Rest Dodd 2: to Satura Crag and Angle Tarn

The distinctive double summit of **ANGLETARN PIKES** *(1857 feet) is a familiar feature high above the Patterdale valley: the two sharp peaks arrest the attention from a distance and are no*

From Angeltarn Pikes 4: Angle Tarn to Patterdale

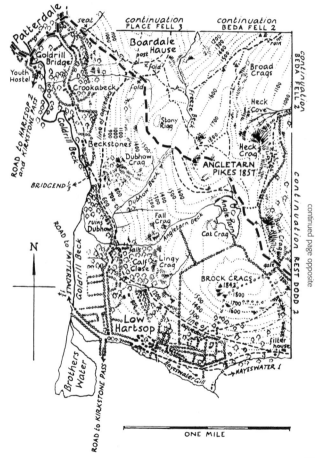

continued page opposite

less imposing on close acquaintance, being attainable only by rock-scrambling, easy or difficult according to choice of route.

The western flank of the fell drops steeply in slopes of bracken to the pleasant strath of Goldrill Beck; on this side, Dubhow Crag and Fall Crag are prominent. More precipitous is the eastern face overlooking the quiet deer sanctuary of Bannerdale where the great bastion of Heck Crag is a formidable object rarely seen by walkers.

Twin upthrusts of rock, 200 yards apart, give individuality to this unusual summit; the northerly is the higher. Otherwise the top is generally grassy, with an extensive peat bog situated in a depression.

Although the view is largely confined by surrounding heights to a five-mile radius, it is full of interest. The abrupt summit gives splendid depth and fall to the prospect south-west where there is a beautiful picture of Brothers Water and Kirkstonefoot. Deepdale, directly below, is especially well seen. The lower summit, south-east, should also be visited; from here there is a charming view back to Angle Tarn but Ullswater cannot be seen.

In mist, there is comfort in knowing that the path for Patterdale is only 100 yards distant down the west slope.

Boardale Hause [spelled Boredale on current OS maps] is a walkers' crossroads, five paths leaving here for different destinations. On the hause is a ruined enclosure resembling a derelict sheepfold, but in fact it is the site of a medieval chapel, as a few carved stones lying around testify. On large-scale maps, this is named as Chapel in the Hause.

Its isolated situation on the ridge, midway between Boardale and Patterdale, was presumably intended to give equal facility of access to the good folk of both valleys. Some years ago, the confusion of paths was further compounded by the construction of an aqueduct across the hause when the pipe-laying operations and tractors carved new routes over the top, but nature is doing its best to remove the scars [and now the only signs are inspection covers which have to be searched for].

There are few fairer scenes than that of the Patterdale valley as seen from the path descending from Boardale Hause. Below is the green strath of cultivated pastures interspersed with mature trees, a sylvan harmony emphasised by the sombre enclosing heights. Brothers Water is glimpsed in the middle distance, and beyond, closing the horizon, Kirkstone Pass.

The path descends into the valley of Patterdale and joins a side road; it finally crosses Goldrill Beck, and the end of the day's march is reached as you enter Patterdale village.

There is an Alpine atmosphere about the little huddle of buildings at Patterdale, and the village, although remote from the heart of the district, conveys the 'feeling' of Lakeland as well as any. It is a place beloved of fellwalkers, the wide choice of routes available on all sides making it a first-rate centre.

Patterdale to St John's in the Vale

Most visitors to Lakeland relate the name of Patterdale to the small village so called near the head of Ullswater, rarely to the delightful valley of which the village is the 'tourist' capital and which gets my vote as the most attractive. Patterdale does have daily visitations of cars and coaches but in fewer numbers than Borrowdale and Langdale, and here it is still possible, especially in early morning and evening, to sense again the absolute quiet and tranquillity of Lakeland a century ago. In Patterdale you can still hear the singing of birds and the murmur of streams above the sound of vehicles. The valley, set deep amongst fells of individual distinction but alike in their invitation, is remarkable for its rapid transition from primeval wildness to pastoral greenery and native woodland, and for its beautiful lake of serpentine curves, which also gets my vote as the fairest of all.

Patterdale village is a centre of excellence for excursions on foot in a lovely countryside. Patterdale seems too good for this poor polluted earth. When I try to visualise heaven, it is not St Peter at the gate and angels sitting on clouds that I see but a paradise modelled on Patterdale with happy hikers on the fells and the Abraham Brothers as gatekeepers.

At the north end of the village is St Patrick's Church,

erected in 1853; since my early visits to the village, the tower has gained a useful but oddly placed clock. I think it looked better without it.

St Patrick's church marks the starting point of a popular route of ascent of Helvellyn. The road into Grisedale leaves the A592 300 yards past the church, rising steadily to the left and ending after a mile.

The path starts half a mile along the road. From this point, the greater part of the approach route to Helvellyn can be prospected: a conspicuous gap in a wall-corner at the top left end of a large enclosure is the next objective. This gap is a mile and a half distant and 1500 ft higher, and obviously will require much time and collar-work to attain. In fact, most of the climbing on the walk occurs within this steep enclosure on the flank of Birkhouse Moor, the unremitting ascent being compensated by impressive views throughout the upper reaches of Grisedale deeply confined by St Sunday Crag and Dollywaggon Pike.

Excitement mounts as the gap in the wall is passed through: there is a feeling that great things are ahead although as yet not fully in view. Gradually the path rises along the crest of steepening cliffs on the left and reaches the foot of an abrupt tower of rock. This has the name of High Spying How but is rarely referred to as such: to walkers coming this way it is the start of Striding Edge.

In clear weather, the dark tower of High Spying How, although still impressive, has no terrors, and a distinct path climbing round its flank brings Striding Edge underfoot and a thrilling prospect ahead.

Striding Edge was long regarded as a fearful place to be avoided, and in icy conditions or gale force winds it can be frightening and indeed quite dangerous. It is Helvellyn's most dramatic feature: a narrow ridge of naked rock, a succession of jagged fangs high above and between very steep and shattered cliffs.

The traverse can be made difficult or easy according to choice: an experienced scrambler on rocks will prefer to make his way along the very crest, but ordinary walkers will use a simple

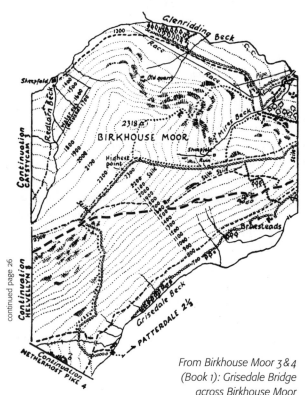

continued opposite

continued page 26

Continuation CATSTYCAM 3

Continuation HELVELLYN 8

Continuation NETHERMOST PIKE 4

From Birkhouse Moor 3&4 (Book 1): Grisedale Bridge across Birkhouse Moor

path running alongside a few feet below. In calm weather, this is an exhilarating adventure with an awkward drop at the far end the only hazard. The Edge is about 300 yards in length and so fascinating that one is tempted to go back and do it again.

In modern times, Striding Edge has become the highlight in the itineraries of countless walkers who, in summer,

continued opposite

have to travel in procession along it; there are even reports of people having to queue to get on it. There is an iron monument on the Edge that may be passed unnoticed: this is the Dixon Memorial, erected in 1858 to mark the scene of a fatal fall during a fox-hunt. The Dixons of those days seem to have been accident-prone; another Dixon fell to his death from the rim of Bleawater Crag on High Street.

The smooth slopes curving up from the west break abruptly along the ridge where, in complete contrast, a shattered cliff of crag and scree falls away precipitously eastwards: here are the most dramatic scenes Helvellyn has to offer. From the edge of the declivity on the summit, Red Tarn is seen directly below, enclosed between the bony arms of Swirral Edge on the left and Striding Edge on the right. Swirral Edge terminates in the grassy cone of Catstycam, a graceful peak, but Striding Edge is all bare rock, a succession of jagged fangs ending in a black tower. The Edges are bounded by deep rough hollows, which are silent and very lonely.

*Having safely negotiated the awkward chimney that terminates Striding Edge, a steep climb on a badly eroded path leads to easy ground on **HELVELLYN**'s broad and grassy top, the point of arrival thereon being at Gough's Memorial erected in 1890 to commemorate a fatal accident in 1803. It is merely now a short*

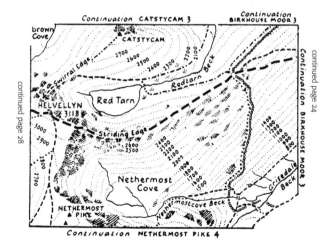

From Helvellyn 8: to Striding Edge and Helvellyn

stroll to a cross-wall built as a shelter from wind and the sum-mit is a few steps beyond (3118 feet).

It might be expected that the summit of so popular a mountain would be crowned with a cairn the size of a house, instead of which the only adornment is a small and insignificant heap of stones that commands no respect at all. This defect is due to the absence of suitable building material on a top covered only by fragments of shale. It is a disappointment to have no cairn to recline against, and as there is no natural seat anywhere on the top, visitors inevitably drift into the nearby wall-shelter. The summit is lacking in natural features, a deficiency which man has attempted to remedy by erecting thereon, as well as the shelter, a triangulation column and two monuments.

Anyone who achieves the summit will be disappointed if the view is obscured by haze but will be delighted in conditions of clear visibility, since the prospect ranges over the whole of Lakeland with all the major peaks splendidly arrayed for inspection. Sunrise visitors must take a chance: a night of stars is often succeeded by banks of mist at dawn.

The view is almost exclusively of mountains, the western horizons in particular being tightly crowded with them, but Ullswater is seen as a silver streak and there is even a glimpse of Morecambe Bay. Most interest will, however, be centred on the more intimate outlook over the eastern flank of the mountain, a dramatic revelation of the coves and ridges abutting against the summit but far below: a harsh landscape better viewed from the edge of the cliffs plunging down to Red Tarn. The Lower Man too commands new vistas and is easily reached.

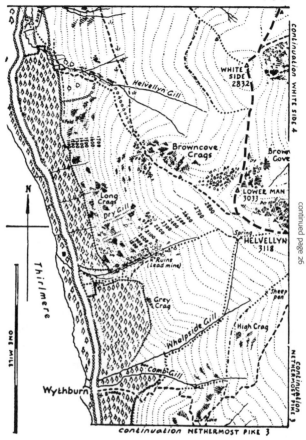

From Helvellyn 7: Helvellyn to White Side

'A savage place', said Wordsworth of this side of Helvellyn and those who look down on it from the top will certainly agree.

Across a shallow depression on the top of Helvellyn and at the edge of the summit plateau is the Lower Man (3033 feet), commanding a view of the range which continues north. It is a prominent object when approached from that direction, indeed appearing to be the true summit. Half a mile on from the principal summit, Lower Man occupies a key position on the main ridge which here changes its direction subtly and unobtrusively. Walkers intending to follow the ridge north may easily go astray hereabouts. The wide path from Helvellyn skirts the Lower Man and continues clearly along a broad spur which appears to be the main ridge (but is, in fact, the direct descent to Thirlspot) while, being indistinct, the bifurcation to the Lower Man may not be noticed, especially in mist.

*From Lower Man, there is a pronounced fall as the main ridge descends to a depression and then rises to the next height in the range, **WHITE SIDE**. This is a name of convenience since the summit (2832 feet) is strictly nameless; White Side is the west slope below the top – probably so called from the splashes of quartz which can be seen on many of the stones.*

The top of White Side is marked by a large cairn set in a wide expanse of excellent turf, with grassy slopes descending gently on all sides. Its sprawling western side is featureless, but it is scarped on the east flank above the now dry bed of Keppelcove Tarn. This was formerly used as a reservoir for the large Greenside Mine but was drained and abandoned when the works closed; the breached dam is one of the few industrial relics remaining in the Helvellyn group. Both sheep and skiers favour White Side.

*A good path leads down from White Side and then rises to the stony summit of **RAISE** (2889 feet).*

continued opposite
and page 34

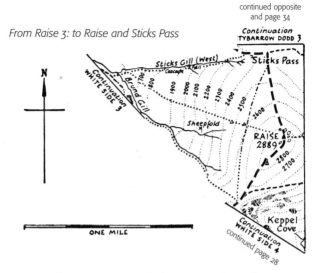

Raise deserves a special cheer. It is the only summit in the Helvellyn range adorned with a crown of rough rocks – and they make a welcome change from the dull monotony of the green expanses around Sticks Pass. But in general the fell conforms to the usual Helvellyn pattern, the western slopes being grassy and a popular winter skiing ground. Midway down its eastern side there was, until recently, an industrial chimney stack marking the end of an underground flue from the Glenridding Lead Mine, which is now closed. The summit of Raise is a level grassy plateau, capped at its higher end by an outcrop of very rough gnarled stones.

I always remember Raise as the fell that gave me the most trouble when I was trying to record the panorama from the summit; eight visits were necessary before I had a day of clear all-round visibility.

The route forwards from Raise is grass all the way after the initial stones. Sticks Pass is, at 2240 ft, the highest pass in Lakeland crossed by a path in common use. The wide summit of the pass was formerly marked by wooden posts, hence the name, but these have now vanished.

NOTE FOR THIS EDITION: Day Two ends by descending Sticks Pass to Stanah in St John's in the Vale.

The descent from the pass is, at first, fairly steep. On your left is the source of Sticks Gill which rises just below Sticks Pass.

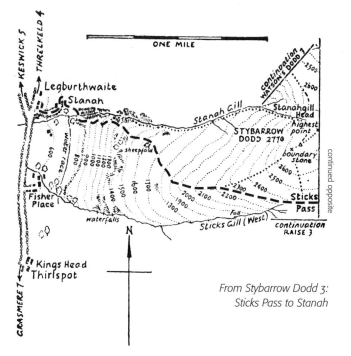

From Stybarrow Dodd 3:
Sticks Pass to Stanah

The bare slopes of Raise, also to your left, are normally unfrequented except when presenting animated scenes in snowy winters, being much favoured by skiers.

The cairned path slopes across an open moor which is the sprawling west slope of Stybarrow Dodd. The gradient increases when the path reaches a sheepfold, and then descends very steeply above the deep ravine of Stanah Gill, a gloomy chasm with many waterfalls.

The gill is crossed by a small bridge, and the path then reaches Stanah, a little group of buildings close to the B5322 which runs through St John's in the Vale.

This road winds through emerald pastures and copses with St John's Beck an ever-present joy; sheep graze happily and undisturbed, and the intervention of man in the rural scenery is restricted to a few neat farmsteads and allotment walls. Everything in the valley breathes contentment.

St John's in the Vale to Scales

NOTE FOR THIS EDITION: Day Three starts by reversing the route of descent taken the day before, and ascending Sticks Pass to the ridge between Raise and Stybarrow Dodd (*see* map on page 31).

A path leaves Stanah, crosses a small bridge, and climbs very steeply above the deep ravine of Stanah Gill. The gradient eases when a sheepfold is reached, the cairned path then slanting across an open moor, the sprawling west slope of Stybarrow Dodd, to overlook the valley of Sticks Gill which is followed up to the source of the stream. The final rise to the summit of the pass is steep. At the top, turn left for Stybarrow Dodd.

Continue up the steepening slope. The boundary stone reached first is usually accepted as the top of **STYBARROW DODD** *(2770 feet) but there is higher ground beyond.*

Stybarrow Dodd is the first of the group of fells north of the Sticks Pass and it sets a pattern for them all: sweeping grassy slopes, easy walking for the traveller who likes to count his miles but rather wearisome for those who prefer to see rock in the landscape. Rock is so rare that the slightest roughnesses get undeserved identification on most maps, either by distinctive name or extravagant hachures: thus Deepdale Crag is hardly more than a short stony slope.

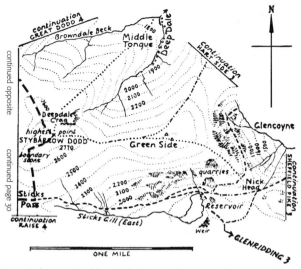

continuation
GREAT DODD 4

continued opposite

continued page 30

continuation
HART SIDE 5

continuation
SHEFFIELD PIKE 5

continuation
RAISE 4

GLENRIDDING 3

Browndale Beck · Middle Tongue · Deep Dale · Deepdale Crag · highest point STYBARROW DODD 2770 · boundary stone · Green Side · Glencoyne · quarries · Nick Head · Sticks Pass · Sticks Gill (East) · Reservoir · Weir

ONE MILE

From Stybarrow Dodd 4: Sticks Pass to beyond Stybarrow Dodd

Stybarrow Dodd sends out a long eastern spur that rises to a minor height, Green Side, before falling steeply to Glencoyne; on Green Side there are both crags and dangerous quarries, now disused.

The route to **WATSON'S DODD** *(2584 feet) is a very easy stroll. A small tarn (often dry) is the only feature. A faint path crosses the depression but does not lead to the summit cairn, which is easily reached by inclining left, slightly ascending across the flat plateau; beware marshy ground.*

Whoever Mr Watson may have been, it is a very odd Dodd that has been selected to perpetuate his name. A separate fell it is undoubtedly, with boundaries unusually sharply defined on north and south by deep ravines, but although it conforms to normal mountain structure on

34

three sides, it has no eastern flank at all. The slope going down east to Deep Dale from the summit plateau is bisected by a stream that clearly divides Great Dodd and Stybarrow Dodd, and Watson's Dodd cannot stake a claim to any land on this side.

A few big stones adorn the highest point, at the western end of the flat triangular top, and they look strangely alien just there in the universal grassiness of the surroundings, as though they had been carried there. (Maybe Mr Watson undertook this task: if so, it is Wtting that the fell should bear his name!) There is a suggestion of history in these hoary stones.

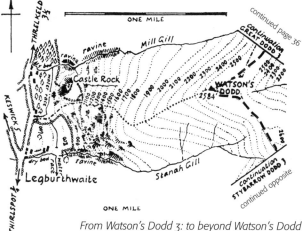

continued page 36

From Watson's Dodd 3: to beyond Watson's Dodd

The route continues to **GREAT DODD** *(2807 feet) by an easy walk on grass.*

Great Dodd, well named, is the most extensive of the fells in the Helvellyn range. To the north-east, its long

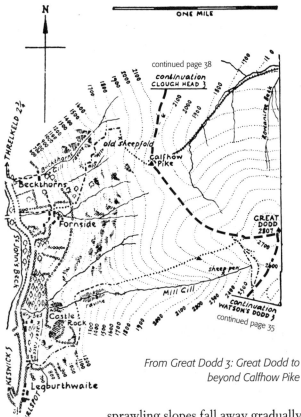

continued page 38

continuation
CLOUGH HEAD 3

Calfhow
Pike

old sheepfold

Beckthorns Gill

THRELKELD 2¼

Beckthorns

Fornside

GREAT
DODD
2807

sheep pen

St JOHN'S BECK

Mill Gill

ravine

continuation
WATSON'S DODD 3
continued page 35

Castle
Rock

KESWICK 5

Legburthwaite

THIRLSPOT

ONE MILE

*From Great Dodd 3: Great Dodd to
beyond Calfhow Pike*

sprawling slopes fall away gradually
in an undulating wilderness of grass to the
old coach-road; north and south, high ground continues the
line of the main ridge, but steepening slopes reach valley-
level on both east and west flanks.

Grass is everywhere: it offers easy and pleasant tramping
but no excitements. Rocks are few and far between: there is

a broken line of cliff, Wolf Crags, overlooking the coach road, and the rough breast of High Brow above Dowthwaitehead breaks out in a series of steep crags (a favourite haunt of buzzards).

[On the north top is the main cairn, which has been constructed since AW produced Book One of the Pictorial Guides.] On the south top is a shelter cairn and the builders must have felt twinges of conscience during their task: they selected as its site a most convenient rash of stones, ignoring the highest point a hundred yards distant, where all is grass except for a naked stone thrusting through the turf, its superior altitude unrecognised. The cairn is hollowed to provide shelter from the west wind.

From Great Dodd the route turns west, then north-west to the curious tor of Calfhow Pike. The path then continues north-north-east to Clough Head; a dull trudge but there are excellent views for compensation.

Contrary to the usual pattern of the Helvellyn fells, of which it is the most northerly member, Clough Head displays its crags to the west and grassy slopes to the east. These crags form a steep, continuous, mile-long wall above St John's in the Vale, with one breach only where a walker may safely venture.

Clough Head is an interesting fell, not only for walkers and explorers but for the ornithologist and botanist, the geologist and antiquarian as well. There is something here for everyone.

*The summit of **CLOUGH HEAD** (2381 feet) is a pleasant grassy sward, adorned with a small wall-shelter and an Ordnance Survey column.*

Clough Head is sufficiently isolated to afford an uninterrupted prospect in every direction except south-east. A special feature, rare in views from the heights of the Helvellyn range, is the nice combination of valley and mountain scenery. This is an excellent viewpoint, the skyline between south and west being exceptionally striking. There is also a superb view of Blencathra directly opposite.

The descent from Clough Head is by White Pike from where the route drops down to Mariel Bridge where a stile gives access

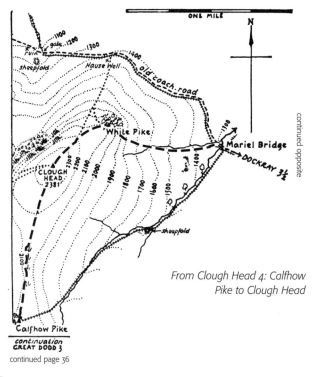

continued opposite

From Clough Head 4: Calfhow Pike to Clough Head

continuation
GREAT DODD 3

continued page 36

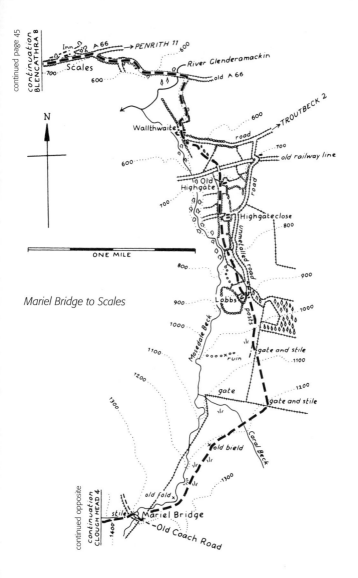

continued page 45

continuation
BLENCATHRA 8

Inn

A 66

→ PENRITH 11

600

Scales

River Glenderamackin

old A 66

600

700

600

N

600

Wallthwaite

road

→ TROUBECK 2

700

old railway line

Old
Highgate

700

road

Highgateclose

800

ONE MILE

800

Unmetalled road

Mariel Bridge to Scales

900

900

Lobbs

1000

Mosedale Beck

posts

1000

ruin

1100

gate and stile

1100

1200

1200

gate

gate and stile

1300

Caral Beck

old bield

1300

continued opposite

continuation
CLOUGH HEAD 4

old fold

stile

Mariel Bridge

1400

Old Coach Road

39

to the Old Coach Road; this is still a public road although rarely used by vehicles nowadays.

A new map (on page 39) shows the route from Mariel Bridge to Scales since this particular stretch, lying between Books One and Five, was not mapped by AW in his Pictorial Guides.

From the old bield, the isolated dome of Great Mell Fell is clearly visible ahead. Aim slightly to the left of this and make for a gate and a stile. The farmhouse of Lobbs was unoccupied in 1992 but still structurally sound. Go through the gateway to Lobbs, but instead of entering the farmyard, bear right to another gate and stile. From here a public footpath leads across the fields to Wallthwaite, passing Highgateclose and Old Highgate, and crossing the disused railway from Penrith to Whitehaven. The road from Wallthwaite to Scales is relatively quiet now that the A66 has been realigned.

NOTE FOR THIS EDITION: Day Three ends at Scales, leaving a short but very energetic day for Day Four.

Scales is only a hamlet, but does have an inn, and is now mercifully by-passed by the busy A66.

Scales to Keswick

NOTE FOR THIS EDITION: Day Four starts at Scales so there is no change to AW's chosen route, only that a whole day has been set aside for the energetic conquest of Blencathra, one of AW's favourite mountains.

Blencathra is one of the grandest mountains in Lakeland and the most imposing of all. It stands in isolation, is strongly individualistic and of unique character. It compels attention even from those people whose eyes are not habitually lifted to the hills. Its supreme feature, the one that endows it with special grandeur, is the very impressive southern front, a remarkable example of the effect of elemental natural forces. This flank forms a tremendous façade above the valley of the Greta, making a dark and towering backcloth to the emerald fields and woodlands, the cottages and farms along its base. There is nothing inviting in these shattered cliffs and petrified rivers of stone that seem to hold a perpetual threat over the community of Threlkeld and the surrounding countryside.

The outer slopes, rising on the west and east flanks from valley level to the uppermost escarpment fringing the summit ridge, are smoothly curved, massive and yet so symmetrical that they might well have been designed by a master architect to supply a perfect balance to the structure. These two outliers are Blease Fell and Scales Fell.

I spent all my leisure time in the winter of 1960–1 exploring Blencathra, thinking about it and writing about it. I climbed all the five ridges and struggled up the four scree-filled watercourses that so deeply divide them. I became familiar with every detail of the topography, scrambling over rough ground where surely no man had trod before, and was completely fascinated by its many ramifications. Never, on any of these wanderings, did I see another person and not even a sheep. This was a no-man's-land in very truth, a steep and inhospitable wilderness, yet, looking down, I could see the busy road only a mile away. I developed a great liking for Blencathra. Familiarity did not bring contempt, only admiration and affection.

The A66 runs along the southern base of Blencathra and travellers on this busy highway get impressive and intimate sightings of the rising buttresses and deep ravines of the lower slopes but, due to foreshortening, only occasional glimpses of the gaunt higher part of the mountain that is called the mountaineers' mountain.

By far the best place for appraising the full extent and unique characteristics of the mountain is Threlkeld Common directly opposite. From here there is a grandstand view of the whole southern façade in detail, a scene of such massive proportions that, even at this distance, a wide-angle lens will be needed for the camera to encompass the full picture, the tumbled walls of an ancient British village adding a foreground interest.

From the high ground of Threlkeld Common the true stature of Blencathra is fully revealed, and the masterly design of its natural architecture can be appreciated.

Having reminded ourselves of the south front of Blencathra, AW's route is now continued, and the ascent of the mountain, via Sharp Edge, starts from Scales.

From Scales there is access to the open fell. Initially the path, made for the ponies of the Victorian pioneers, goes to the right above the intake wall and then mounts the slope towards Mousthwaite Comb. The path continues into the valley of the River Glenderamackin (while the path which rises to Doddick Fell forks off to the left) until reaching Scales Beck which is then followed upstream to Scales Tarn.

The immense hollow on the eastern flank, scooped out of the fellside as though by a giant bulldozer, was shaped by a retreating glacier in millennia long past, leaving a debris of crags and scree, a petrified desert without life or movement, pervaded by an awesome stillness. This dead landscape is relieved of its solemnity by a sheet of water, Scales Tarn, deeply inurned below a crescent of impending crags and steep declivities and serving as a natural reservoir for the drainage from the slopes of the recess. The tarn occupies a pleasant grassy basin but under a grey sky appears sullen and gloomy and rather sinister; only the lapping of water on the shores and the gurgle of the outflow into Scales Beck disturb the profound silence.

From Scales Tarn, the slope to the right leads up to Sharp Edge; this is traversed to reach the Saddle on a much-eroded path, finally passing the white cross to the summit. Sharp Edge

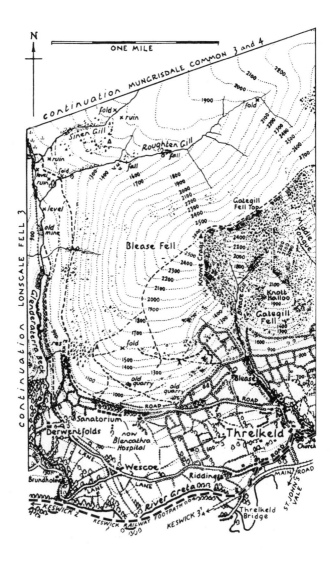

N

ONE MILE

continuation MUNGRISDALE COMMON 3 and 4

fold ×
× ruin
fold

2100
2000
1900

2800

Siden Gill
Roughten Gill
fall

2200
2300
2400
2500
2700

× ruin
level
ruin
fold
fall
1600
1700

1800
1900
2000
2100
2300
2400
2500

Gategill Fell Top

Middle Tongue

× level

2200
2400
2200
2000
1800

old mine
900

Blease Fell

2500
2400
2300
2200
2100
2000
1900
1800

Knowe Crags

2100
Knott Halloo

Gategill Fell
1400
1500
1600

continuation LONSCALE FELL 3

Glenderaterra Beck

fold

1700
1600
1500
1400
1300
1100
1000

old quarry
old quarry

1700
900

Blease

ROAD

700

Sanatorium
Derwentfolds
now
Blencathra
Hospital

700

Threlkeld

Church

LANE

Wescoe
Riddings
River Greta

KESWICK 2
KESWICK RAILWAY FOOTPATH
KESWICK 3¾

Brundholme
LANE

MAIN ROAD
ST. JOHN'S VALE

Threlkeld
Bridge

44

From Blencathra 7–8 (Book 5): from Scales to the summit of Blencathra and the descent to Threlkeld

Map labels: 2700, 2400, 2100, old mine, fold, CONTINUATION BANNERDALE CRAGS 3, 1700, 1600, 1500, MUNGRISDALE 2, Foule Crag, Sharp Edge, Tarn Crags, 2000, River Glenderamackin, 1500, 1400, 1300, CONTINUATION SOUTHER FELL 4, Scales Tarn, 1700, BLENCATHRA 2847, Hallsfell Top, Doddick Fell Top, 2200, 1800, Mousthwaite Combe, Scales Fell, Doddick Gill, Goat Crags, 1200, Scaley Beck, 1100, Scales, PENRITH 113, Doddick Fell, 1200, 1100, access to fell, 700, Doddick, Hall's Fell, 1100, 1000, MAIN ROAD, Gategill, old mine workings, old levels, Gate Gill, old levels

continued page 39

is the magnet that attracts many walkers to this interesting, if awkward, route. Sharp Edge is well named: it juts from the main mass of the mountain below the Saddle as a narrow spine of rock bristling with vertebrae in the form of pinnacles and towers of intimidating aspect. In some ways it resembles the better-known Striding Edge on Helvellyn but it is shorter and, if the crest is traversed from end to end without deviation, is much more difficult and dangerous.

To the early Victorian pioneers, Sharp Edge was a terrifying place and its crossing perilous; this is not so today if advantage is taken of a pedestrian path formed by the passage of many

boots on the northern side of the crest and a few feet below it.
The sides of Sharp Edge are steep and in places precipitous so
that it is advisable to walk circumspectly and keep strictly to the
trodden path. There is one minor difficulty at the point where the
Edge abuts the fellside, where a small tilted slab has to be nego-
tiated: here the ultra-cautious walker, decorum abandoned,
will prefer to shuffle across the impasse in a sitting position.
Otherwise there is nowadays nothing to fear when traversing
the Edge in fair conditions; when wet, extra care is needed;
when sheathed in ice, it is far better avoided.

Sharp Edge is exciting, exhilarating and a memorable
adventure.

From the end of the Edge, the walk continues up the side of
Foule Crag, and up towards the Saddle. Although poised high
above a shattered landscape, it provides the easiest walking sur-
face on the mountain, a simple stroll on excellent turf.

Walkers who reach the depression of the Saddle will be
curious to learn about a man-made and unique landmark
they will see there. A cross has been laid out on the ground,
composed of white crystallised stones of high quartz content. Locals believe it was originally intended to be a
memorial to a walker who died when walking on the mountain, but its initial small size has been extended to its present
proportions of 16ft × 10ft. A Threlkeld man, Harold Robinson, climbed Blencathra, his favourite mountain, hundreds
of times and, on each visit, he added a few more stones from
the nearby veins of quartzite. The cross may now be
regarded as a memorial to Mr Robinson too.

An untidy pile of stones marks the summit of **BLENCATHRA**
(2847 feet) and is surrounded by a greensward that invites rest

and a contemplation of the magnificent panorama revealed on all sides.

The views are far reaching, extending to distant horizons except where interrupted by the greater bulk of nearby Skiddaw. Over the lesser northern fells is seen the Solway plain and eastwards, in a wealth of detail, is the Penrith countryside and the fertile Eden Valley backed by the highest of the Pennines with Cross Fell overtopping the range. Towards the south, the fells of Lakeland start to erupt from their lovely valleys, culminating in the massive upthrust of Helvellyn and its supporting satellites. But it is in the arc between south and south-west that attention will be mostly riveted: here is a tumult of peaks so crowded together that the identification of each can only be made by fellwalkers with a long and intimate knowledge of the district. This is a compelling vista, a picture of infinite beauty, and in its midst like a jewel in a prickly crown, is Derwentwater.

NOTE FOR THIS EDITION: There are a number of routes leading from the summit of Blencathra to Threlkeld which fit the 2 miles designated by AW in his original list; Hall's Fell has been selected since it leads directly from the summit.

The Ordnance Survey prefer to name the summit Hallsfell Top and, indeed, it is situated precisely where Hall's Fell abuts on the summit ridge. But those who reach this exalted peak do not record in their diaries 'Climbed Hallsfell Top today': they say 'Climbed Blencathra today'. Hall's Fell takes its name from Threlkeld Hall, which is set in fields on the other side of the A66 in the valley.

A path leads from the summit via a slender ridge to Narrow Edge which is an exhilarating section. It is so-called with good reason: Narrow Edge — poised high between the depths of Gate Gill and Doddick Gill — is a succession of low crags, with steps and gateways and towers of rock. A distinct track on grass is available for walkers — at first this keeps to the right side of the ridge, later on the left, the Doddick Gill side; occasionally, it is forced along the crest. Care is needed but there are no difficulties. Scramblers will enjoy following the crest throughout — but under ice and snow, the ridge is for experts only.

At the end of the ridge, the gradient eases for a while and then follows a steepish but enchanting track downwards through heather and bracken to reach Gategill. The path joins the lane which served the old Gategill Mine (now disused), then passes Woodend Mine (also disused) to reach the lane which turns right for Threlkeld. Alternatively, take a footpath south-west from Gategill to reach the village.

Here look over both parapets of Threlkeld Bridge. Two streams, the River Glenderamackin and St John's Beck, at this point unite, passing under the bridge individually but emerging as one: the River Greta. The bridge is built over the confluence.

AW's list indicated that, from Thelkeld, a bus should be taken into Keswick. In the present day, there are of course fewer buses and more cars. Walkers wishing to complete the link to the next day's start can take the footpath which follows the old railway track for the final three miles into Keswick.

Keswick to Buttermere

Keswick has changed since my early visits before the war and I am not a lone voice in saying that the town had a greater appeal in the old days when there were far fewer visitors and a man with a rucksack on his back was an object of curiosity. There were few cars, the usual form of travel was by Ribble bus; the only places of refreshment for those of us not sufficiently affluent to patronise the hotels were the Grey Friars Café and Dalzell's chip shop.

On days too wet for the fells, steps gravitated to the photographic galleries of the Abraham Brothers, where the high places were portrayed in magnificent camera studies that have never been surpassed or even equalled.

After the war, Keswick gradually became too tourist-conscious for my liking; new cafés and gift shops sprouted, car parks were provided and too many people who now came were not fellwalkers or admirers of the scenery but ice-cream suckers disgorged from coaches.

But no happenings in Keswick's emergence as a tourist magnet can detract from the glory of the countryside around. The town is exceptionally favoured by its location in a wide strath of verdant pastures and woodlands. It lies within a sheltering circle of mountains and fells draped in tapestries of rich colour, with Derwentwater a glittering jewel in their midst. And standing guard over this precious heritage, as he has done faithfully and proudly since rising from the sea millions of years ago, is dear old Skiddaw.

Leave Keswick by the Cockermouth road, and immediately after crossing the River Greta take a footpath on the left that leads to the old road from Keswick to Portinscale. Turn left into the road, crossing the River Derwent by a pedestrian suspension bridge, and keep straight on through the village of Portinscale. About 25 yards beyond the lane to Nichol End, a gap in the beech hedge on the left admits to a wood. In less than a mile the path enters the area shown on the map, crosses the road to Hawse End and joins the road from Portinscale to Grange at a bend. The path to **CATBELLS** *leaves from the road junction ahead, doubles back to the left and joins the path coming up from the car park.*

The name Catbells might well be a corruption of Cat Bields (the shelter of the wildcat) although this has been disputed by authorities of repute. It is interesting to note, however, that the crags below the top on the west side have the name of Mart Bield (the shelter of the marten), which seems to lend support to the suggestion.

Catbells is one of the great favourites, a family fell where grandmothers and infants can climb the heights together, a place beloved. Its popularity is well-deserved: its shapely topknot attracts the eye, offering a steep but obviously simple scramble to the small summit; its slopes are smooth, sunny and sleek; its position overlooking Derwentwater is superb. Moreover, for strong walkers it is the first step on a glorious ridge that bounds Borrowdale on the west through-out its length with Newlands down on the other side.

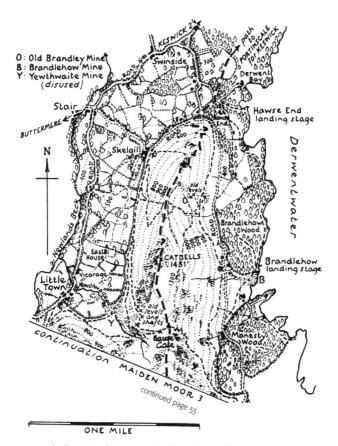

continued page 53

ONE MILE

From Catbells 4 (Book 6): to Catbells and on to Hause Gate

Yet this fell is not quite so innocuous as is usually thought, and grandmothers and infants should have a care as they romp around. There are some natural hazards in the form of a line of crags that starts at the summit and slants down to Newlands, and steep outcrops everywhere. More dangerous are the levels and open shafts that pierce the fell on both flanks.

Words cannot adequately describe the rare charm of Catbells, nor its ravishing view. But no publicity is necessary: its mere presence in the Derwentwater scene is enough. It has a bold 'come hither' look that compels one's steps, and no suitor ever returns disappointed, but only looking back often.

The summit of Catbells, which has no cairn, is a small platform of naked rock, light brown in colour and seamed and pitted with many tiny hollows and crevices that collect and hold rain-water – so that, long after the skies have cleared, glittering diamonds adorn the crown. Almost all the native vegetation has been scoured away by the varied footgear of countless visitors; so popular is this fine view-point that often it is difficult to find a vacant perch. In summer, this is not a place to seek quietness.

After the summit of Catbells (1481 feet), the next objective is Maiden Moor. A slight depression must first be crossed and this is Hause Gate.

There is, of course, no gate at Hause Gate, just as there is no door at Mickle Door. 'Gate' and 'door' are local geographical terms for a way or opening through the hills or across a ridge. 'Hause' is another good Lakeland name for a pass. 'Hause Gate' is therefore really a tautological name.

*From Hause Gate, a track veering to the right mounts steadily to **MAIDEN MOOR**, aiming for a low cairn that appears to be the summit, but isn't. This cairn is a viewpoint par excellence: it commands an out-of-this world prospect of*

Derwentwater backed by Blencathra, a scene that nobody carrying a camera can possibly resist.

Short of lying down with eyes at ground level and taking a few elementary perspectives, there is no way by which a layman can determine the highest point of the fell – and although the Ordnance Survey have been on the spot with instruments and arrived at their own expert conclusions (1887 feet), they have left no sign of their visit, and there is no cairn. The actual top could be anywhere within a

continued page 51

continued page 55

From Maiden Moor 3: Hause Gate to Blea Crag

twenty-yard radius. All is grassy and uninteresting here, without as much as a stone to sit on or an outcrop to recline against.

Maiden Moor is on the spine of the ridge forming the Newlands and Borrowdale watershed. Both flanks are scarped – that facing Newlands almost continuously – so that, while the walk along the top is simple and pleasant, on grass, direct access from either valley is a possibility only in a few places without encountering rock.

The route from Maiden Moor to High Spy is an excellent ridge walk. The path becomes unexpectedly very good as it crosses Narrow Moor and climbs up beyond; it is obviously engineered, perhaps built for ponies. Crags on the right add an increasing interest to the later stages of the walk. The short detour to the cairn on Blea Crag is strongly urged: here is one of the finest views of Derwentwater.

Interest along the ridge to High Spy is sustained by the succession of cliffs and arêtes falling away abruptly from the crest to the desolate upper Newlands valley, for on this western flank there is no wide plateau but, in contrast, the appalling mile-long precipice known to the rock-climbing fraternity as Eel Crags.

The growing popularity of rock-climbing during the last few decades has led to the development as climbing grounds of crags that had hitherto not been considered worthy of serious attention. The mile-long façade of Eel Crags now yields several good routes.

HIGH SPY *above the valley of Newlands is well named. From its rocky top there is a far-reaching view across the district with mountain range succeeding mountain range to end with*

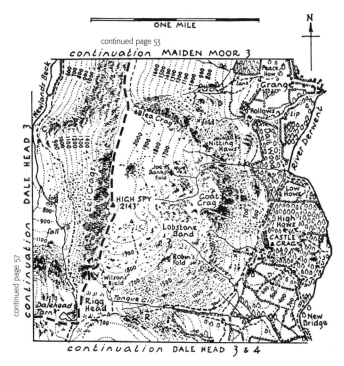

continued page 53

ONE MILE

N

continuation MAIDEN MOOR 3

Newlands Beck

Peace How

Grange

Hollows

River Derwent

Blea Crag

Fold

Nitting Haws

continuation DALE HEAD 3

Joe K Banks Fold

Eel Crags

Goat Crag

Low Hows

HIGH SPY
▲ 2143'

Lobstone Band

High Hows

CASTLE CRAG

continued page 57

800·
900·
fall
1100

Robin's Fold

Wilson's Bield

Tongue Gill

Dalehead Tarn

Rigg Head

R

New Bridge

continuation DALE HEAD 3 & 4

From High Spy 4: to High Spy and Dalehead Tarn

Helvellyn on the eastern horizon. The summit cairn (2143 feet) is a solid, well-built structure, the result of diligent toil: a memorial to its unknown builders.

The view is extensive and generally good, the main interest being centred in the south where the Scafell group captures attention and Great Gable is especially prominent. As a viewpoint, the cairn is a little too far from the edge of the precipice to add drama to the scene, but there are several places nearby where profound glimpses down into the wild recesses of upper Newlands may be obtained.

There is now movement from one ridge to another, and costly in time and effort. Go down to Rigg Head on an improving cairned path with impressive crags on the right and continue ahead until Dalehead Tarn, hidden by rocky tors, appears on the right.

Dale Head's greatest triumph over its north-western fellows is that it holds in its lap the only tarn of any size between Bassenthwaite and Honister, a manifestation of the change in the underlying rock.

*The shortest ascent to the summit of **DALE HEAD** starts from the far end of Dalehead Tarn, there being a track for most of the way. This climb is steep and, like all climbs, longer than expected.*

I well remember, in the days when I was a raw apprentice on the hills, ill-prepared and ill-equipped, toiling up this slope in a state of near exhaustion: there was no track then and the ascent seemed interminable; for the last few hundred yards I was reduced to crawling upwards on hands and knees. As always on the hills, a five-minute halt was enough to restore sufficient energy to enable me to go on my way. In those far-off days, too, my routine was to descend steep grass by shuffling down on my bottom, a practice I still adopt on occasion because a tough and rubbery bottom is a valuable agent of friction, a sheet anchor with superb resistance to the pull of gravity. Once this method of downward progression ended in calamity when a concealed rock neatly removed the seat of my pants, a matter of indifference while I was alone in the hills but in

the streets of Keswick later, and on the bus going home, I
had to hide my embarrassed flesh in a buttoned-up plastic
raincoat although the day was sunny and warm and everybody else was in shirt sleeves. Since then, my advice to
others is to keep the body erect when walking steeply
up or down.

Dale Head was
obviously named
by the early
settlers

continued page 60

continuation HINDSCARTH 4

continuation HINDSCARTH 4

continuation HIGH SPY 4

continued page 12

*From Dale Head 3:
Rigg Head to
beyond Dale Head*

in Newlands: it effectively terminates the upper reaches of that lovely valley, appearing as an immense barrier of forbidding cliffs in perpetual shadow, yet proving a good friend as a provider of the stream that nurtures the fertile pastures and meadows of Newlands, and the mineral wealth that for centuries sustained the local economy. Today Dale Head is an industrial graveyard, a mouldering museum of relics of former activity, a place haunted by the ghosts of men who once laboured here. I am always saddened when I see ruins, especially those in lonely places where conditions must have been primitive. I find myself trying to imagine the folk who lived and worked there in happier days with no thoughts of the fate that was to befall them, of the heartbreak of their final departure, taking their memories and leaving behind so much to rot and decay. Ruins are the burial grounds of hopes and aspirations.

Dale Head is not usually classed amongst the grandest of Lakeland's fells and is seldom the sole objective of an expedition: indeed, its modest altitude (2473 feet) precludes its admission to the ranks of the greatest. It has much in common with Eel Crag in the Grasmoor group. Their summits are focal points of high country, the meeting place of ascending ridges. Both have craggy northern fronts, darkly shadowed, and easy southern approaches. Both enjoy extensive views of great merit, particularly northwards to Skiddaw. Taking everything into account these two may be considered the most satisfying summits in the north-western area.

Dale Head has interest for the geologist, for beneath the carpet of grass there is a fusion of the Skiddaw slates and the volcanic rock of central Lakeland, some evidence of the join being seen on the actual summit. Streams flow in all directions, except west, yet it is in the west their ultimate destiny lies, the fell being wholly within the catchment of the Derwent.

The toil of the ascent is immediately forgotten on arrival at the summit. In every direction the panorama is magnificent, especially excelling in the full-length view of Newlands, the wild upper valley merging into the sylvan scenery beyond, and distant Skiddaw closing the picture perfectly. This I consider to be the finest aerial view of a valley from a Lakeland summit.

There are hundreds of unnecessary cairns on the fells, and no great loss would be suffered if they were scattered, but those on the summits of the mountains have a special significance: they are old friends and should be left inviolate in their lonely stations to greet their visitors. The summit of Dale Head is a simple mound with a magnificent cairn of slate built by a professional craftsman, a work of art that should be revered as much as a monument in a churchyard. Its situation is dramatic, immediately on the brink of the great northern downfall, but there is an easy parade on both sides.

From Dale Head a path leads west alongside the few surviving posts of an old fence and descends gradually to a narrow depression beyond which the fence is left for a beeline trek to the summit of Hindscarth in the north, this lying half a mile off the direct course.

Hindscarth is a twin to Robinson. Both were created in the same upheaval and sculptured in the same mould. They turn broad backs to the Buttermere valley and go hand-in-hand together down to Newlands, their ridges reaching the valley at the beautiful watersmeet near the little church. The eastern flank

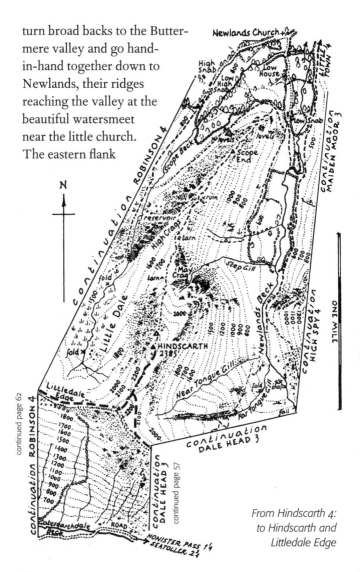

From Hindscarth 4:
to Hindscarth and
Littledale Edge

continued page 62

continued ROBINSON 4

continued page 57

of Hindscarth falls very roughly and steeply into the upper Newlands valley, draining to the fell's main watercourse, Newlands Beck, which goes on to join the Derwent.

*The top of **HINDSCARTH** is a full half-mile in length, the contours gently building up to the highest point (2385 feet), near the north-east end, where a cairn stands amongst embedded rocks. Elsewhere the summit is grassy, with patches of gravel.*

Continuing the line of the ridge, and 200 paces away, on the edge of the north-east declivity, there is a big circular cairn of some antiquity, the Ordnance Survey maps giving it distinction by the use of the lettering reserved for objects of historic interest. This is the cairn prominently seen from Newlands, and it commands the finest view from the mountain. The interior is hollowed out to provide a windshelter.

One of the delights of fellwalking on the north-western fells is the splendid views from their summits and high ridges of the greater heights to the south. Hindscarth is well favoured in this respect having a wide panorama ranging from Bowfell and the Scafell range to Great Gable.

Hindscarth and Robinson are lateral spurs springing from the right of the north wall of Gatesgarthdale, and a beeline between the two summits is out of the question since Little Dale lies deeply between the summits of Hindscarth and Robinson and can only be circumvented by using the fenced ridge to the south, Littledale Edge. The ridge has five features in a regular pattern. On the ridge is the path, bounded by a fence, over which is a shallow escarpment with a fringe of scree contained by a ruined wall. All these occur in a narrow strip over a considerable distance to, across and beyond a grassy depression. This depression is remarkable and an interest can be added to the climb there from by a short detour over the fence to look at the strange formation known as Hackney Holes and Robinson Crags. Watch for the conspicuous end of a broken wall (which looks like a cairn from the road below) – since this stands on the rim of the main hole. Some care is needed in exploration.

The fell with the prosaic name of Robinson is the least attractive of the group which surrounds Buttermere, a defect largely due to its position on the sunny side of the valley. Lack of shadow always reduces the visual appeal of mountain scenery, and on Robinson the steep slopes rise blandly to the sky with nothing in particular to attract the eye, nothing to exercise the curiosity and imagination – in complete contrast to the darkly mysterious and more challenging heights across the lake. One must see it from Newlands to appreciate its distinctive skyline and the long ridge that characterises this aspect, its finest; while from Newlands Hause, too, it is strongly in evidence, here fringed by the half-mile precipice of Robinson Crags.

It's a pity about the name which derives from a Richard Robinson who purchased estates, including this unnamed fell, at Buttermere many centuries ago; thereafter it was known as 'Robinson's Fell'. But it could have been worse: this early land speculator might have been a Smith or a Jones – or a Wainwright.

*Two long low outcrops of rock run parallel across the summit (2417 feet) of **ROBINSON**, the width of a road apart, almost like natural kerbstones or parapets – the westerly is slightly the higher and has the main cairn. The 'road' between is surfaced with loose stones. The top of the fell is a broad plateau with*

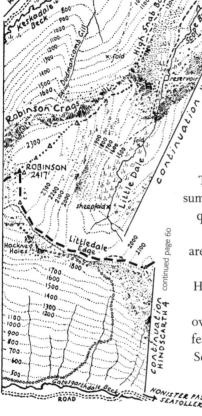

continuation KNOTT RIGG 2

Keskadale Beck

800

900
1000
1100
Ddd.n.omb Gill
1200
1300
1400
1500
1600

Robinson Crag

2300

▲ ROBINSON
2417'

2300
2200
2100
2000

sheepfold ×

fold ×

High Snab Bank

reservoir

Scope Beck

800
900
1000
1100

900
1000
1100
1200
1300
1400
1500

fold

Little Dale

continuation HINDSCARTH 4

continued page 60

2000
2100

Littledale Edge

Hackney Holes

1700
1600
1500
1400
1300
1200
1100
1000
900
800
700
600
500

Gatesgarthdale Beck

ROAD

continuation HINDSCARTH 4

HONISTER PASS 1¼
SEATOLLER 2½

N
↑
ONE MILE

continued page 65

From Robinson 4: Littledale Edge to Robinson

nothing of interest and no hazards. This broad, nearly flat summit detracts from the quality of the view but although the valleys are hidden the surround of fells is excellent. Honister Pass, with the motor road snaking over it, is an interesting feature. It is odd to find Scafell Pike's towering summit for once missing from a view, especially as all its satellites are there in force: the Pike is exactly covered by the top of Great Gable, but its south-west slope going down to the gap of Mickledore is clearly visible. Robinson is one of the few fells that has the shy Floutern Tarn in its sights.

From the summit of Robinson, the path – gentle in descent at first and then steep above the scree – leads down on the left of Robinson Crags. The scree is crossed by a grass tongue. There is a perfect view ahead of Loweswater cradled in its fells.

Since Book 6 of the Pictorial Guides was compiled, a path has been established between Buttermere Moss and Newlands Hause.

The route now crosses Buttermere Moss; keep to the right edge of the Moss to avoid wet ground. There is a fine view on the right to High Hole which is a small but excellent specimen of a hanging valley halting a downfall of crags. Go over Moss Beck which, considering the apparent volume of Moss Force, is small, running in a deep, narrow channel and may be crossed by a stride. The path now skirts the crags on the right in a series of interesting ʒig-ʒags and then shortly reaches Newlands Hause.

Newlands Hause, often wrongly referred to as Buttermere Hause, carries a narrow motor road, non-commercial and normally quiet but much used by summer and weekend visitors to the district. The top of the pass provides parking space for the many cars halting there.

NOTE FOR THIS EDITION: This section of the walk, which was AW's Third Day, has been split into two, and the first half ends here at Newlands Hause. Those doing the Memorial Walk in its entirety are advised to turn left and make their way to the village of Buttermere which can be their base for the next two nights.

The road, on its long decline to Buttermere (1½ miles away) is not exclusively the preserve of motorists, and walkers can and

continued page 62

often
do use it,
but there is
little opportunity
to escape the hard
unyielding surface.

The village of Buttermere, to its credit, has remained as sweet and unspoiled as when I first saw it and, despite an increasing influx of visitors,

From Robinson 3: across
Buttermere Moss to Newlands
Hause and Buttermere

as charming. Long may it remain so. Blessed by an idyllic setting in the shelter of majestic fells, Buttermere is a foretaste of heaven. And its shining jewel is its lovely lake, mirror of an enchanting landscape.

The Buttermere Circuit

NOTE FOR THIS EDITION: Those who stayed in the village of Buttermere overnight need to retrace their footsteps of the previous evening, walking the 1½ miles back to Newlands Hause.

The ascent of Knott Rigg from Newlands Hause is a simple and straightforward climb on the sunny side of the Hause. Start anywhere across the gentle alp on the north side of the pass. From the little hollow beyond, the thin track climbing up to the ridge can be seen ahead.

An advantage of solitary travel on the fells, greatly appreciated by all lone walkers, is the freedom to perform a certain function as and where one wishes, without any of the consultation and subterfuges necessitated by party travel. The narrow crest of Knott Rigg is no place for indulging the practice, however, whether alone or accompanied, walkers here being clearly outlined against the sky and in full view from two valleys. This comment is intended for males particularly. Women (according to an informant) have a different way of doing it.

Beyond the last outcrop, the excellent turf of the ridge gives place to tougher grass, the summit being reached across a marshy plateau. Upon reaching the ridge, there is at once a fine view down the other side to Sail Beck and across it to the tremendous scarred wall of Wandope, Eel Crag and Sail.

*The summit of **KNOTT RIGG** (1790 feet), a grassy mound, lies 400 yards beyond the official highest point, across a marsh, and overlooking the valley of Sail Beck.*

Knott Rigg is so tightly sandwiched between the impending masses of Robinson and the Eel Crag range that an extensive view is not to be expected. The distant scene is not completely restricted, however, and eastwards there is a glorious outlook across the valley of Newlands to the lofty skyline of Helvellyn and the Dodds.

continued page 68

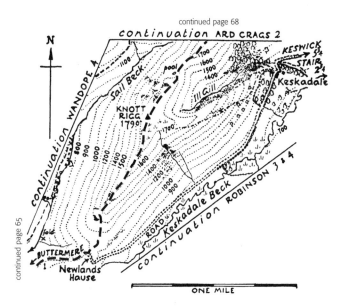

From Knott Rigg 2: Newlands Hause to beyond Knott Rigg

*There is little fall in height for a furlong or so on the path to Ard Crags, which then follows a gradual descent to a hollow occupied by a patch of gravel and a pond (sometimes dry). Thereon a better path rises through heather to **ARD CRAGS**.*

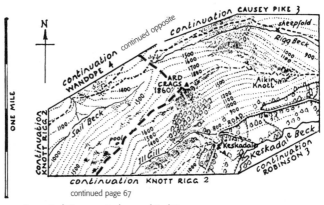

continued page 67

From Ard Crags 2: to beyond Ard Crags

The fell of Ard Crags is commonly referred to as Aikin Knott, which is more properly the name of a rocky excrescence on the 1500-feet contour. Save a visit here for a warm still day in August and envy not the crowds heading for Great Gable. The narrow crest is a dense carpet of short springy heather, delightful to walk upon and even better as a couch for rest and meditation. But slumber is a hazard, for crags fall away sharply below one's boots to Keskadale. The highest point, marked by a cairn [now just a very low pile of stones], has no official altitude, the surveyors having preferred to adopt the eastern end of the summit, at 1821 feet, for their use. [In fact, the latest OS 1:25 000 map gives an altitude of 1906 feet.]

The highlight of the view is the beautiful detail of Newlands, a picture of bright pastures intermingled with heathery ridges, backed by the Helvellyn range, which is seen end to end in the distance. In other directions, nearby higher fells seriously curtail the view, and this is especially so between west and north, where the massive wall of the Eel Crag range towers above, impressively close.

*At Ard Crags the route makes a right-angled turn to the left and descends to a pass. On the far side of the pass a patch of green marks the position of a spring. A few yards above the spring, a path will be found rising to the right up to Sail Pass. Sail Pass is a name of convenience; there is no official name. Instead of continuing on the path which leads to Newlands, a left turn is taken to head for the next objective, **SAIL**.*

Sail is the least obtrusive of the 2500-footers, being completely dominated by its vaster and more rugged neighbour, Eel Crag, and an absence of attractive or interesting features adds to its inferiority complex. Sail is, however, an unavoidable obstacle on the way to or from the bigger fell by the fine east ridge rooted in Newlands, and the well-trodden path to its

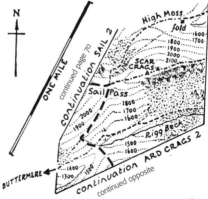

From Causey Pike 3:
the route to Sail Pass

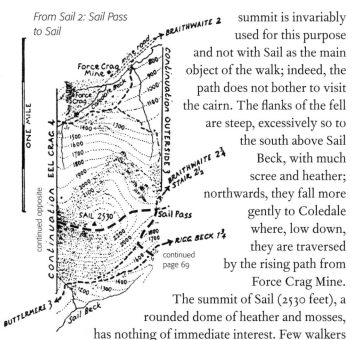

*From Sail 2: Sail Pass
to Sail*

BRAITHWAITE 2

Force Crag
Mine

mine road

continuation OUTERSIDE 3

800
900
1000
1100

Force
Crag

Coledale Beck

ONE MILE

continuation EEL CRAG 4

1200
1300
1400
1500
1600
1700
1800
1900
2000
2100

BRAITHWAITE 2¾
STAIR 2½

continued opposite

SAIL 2530'

Sail Pass

2200
2100
2000

1800
1700

RIGG BECK 1¼

continued
page 69

continuation

1600
1500

1400
1200
1300

BUTTERMERE 3

Sail Beck

summit is invariably
used for this purpose
and not with Sail as the main
object of the walk; indeed, the
path does not bother to visit
the cairn. The flanks of the fell
are steep, excessively so to
the south above Sail
Beck, with much
scree and heather;
northwards, they fall more
gently to Coledale
where, low down,
they are traversed
by the rising path from
Force Crag Mine.

The summit of Sail (2530 feet), a
rounded dome of heather and mosses,
has nothing of immediate interest. Few walkers
will hesitate long over this panorama, with the better viewpoint of Eel Crag so near, but those who cannot go a step
further without a rest may settle down to enjoy what is
really a very fine prospect, although unbalanced by the dis-
proportionate bulk of Eel Crag filling the western sky.

*An easy 100-ft drop to the connecting depression (which is
not a pass) is the prelude to an exhilarating climb up the narrow crest with two rocky rises to the broad top of **EEL CRAG**.
Here the path (which has been clear throughout) fades away,
but the summit (2749 feet) is close at hand and reached by bearing half-right.*

The Ordnance Survey persists in naming this mountain Crag Hill, and although it must be assumed that they are correct in doing so, their choice of name has never been generally accepted, Eel Crag being preferred by most guide-book writers and walkers. Jenkinson's guidebook, which was written in the middle of last century, and Baddeley's more recent one, both described it as Eel Crag without mention of Crag Hill as an option and it is as Eel Crag that the mountain is popularly known. Even this is a misnomer, however, since the cliffs of the undisputed Eel Crag are half

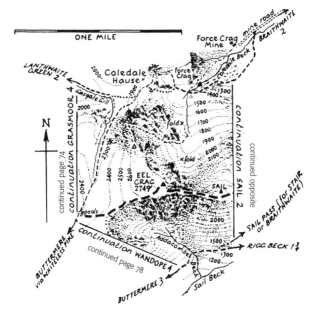

From Eel Crag 4: Sail to beyond Eel Crag

a mile distant from the summit and overlook Coledale Hause.

The mountain is best viewed from Coledale where it dominates the head of the valley. It also presents a tremendous broadside to the deep trench of Sail Beck, but apart from these aspects it lacks distinction of outline and despite its impressive bulk does not have the magnetic appeal of other more shapely heights in Lakeland. Nevertheless, it is of strategic importance geographically as the hub of a group of fells, a watershed of streams draining both north and south, although all are within the gathering grounds of the River Derwent. It is buttressed by ascending ridges from Newlands and Buttermere.

The great feature of the mountain is the north-east flank, steeply descending in a wild confusion of crags and outcrops and runs of scree that repel exploration; the south face, too, is defended by a line of cliffs and only westwards is there a simple slope of easy gradient. In the south, between Eel Crag and the neighbouring height of Wandope, is a vast hollow of special interest, a perfect example of a hanging valley to which the contours of the Ordnance Survey maps do not do justice: this is Addacomb Hole where a great scoop gouged out of the fellside is halted midway on its fall to Sail Beck.

Eel Crag is the pivot of the north-western fells and is the greatest influence in the surrounding landscape but is not the highest point, that honour going to Grasmoor, a compelling and more readily identifiable object only a mile away in the west and linked by an ascending ridge, but Grasmoor stands alone and it is to Eel Crag that the fells of Whiteless Pike,

Wandope, Sail and Causey Pike have an affinity. Eel Crag is the head of a family; Grasmoor is without kin.

The highest point is distinguished by an Ordnance Survey column, but is otherwise unpretentious, being rather flat. It is a place to halt and admire a diverse panorama but bear in mind that wandering around the top is severely restricted by cliffs immediately east and south.

The view is almost exclusively of mountains and fells, these forming the horizon in all directions; the southern skyline is particularly impressive. Lakes and tarns are not much in evidence and it is disappointing to find the nearby lakes of Buttermere and Crummock Water concealed from sight by intervening fells.

*To reach **GRASMOOR** from Eel Crag, there is a long moorland tramp of approximately 1¼ miles. Go down the easy slope west to cross the Coledale Hause–Whiteless Pike path near two small pools. Beyond, follow a rising line of cairns up the grassy breast to the vast, gently rising top of Grasmoor, the main cairn of which is still a further half-mile distant.*

Grasmoor is the giant of the north-western fells in terms of feet and inches (2791 feet) but superior height alone is not always a measure of importance. As is the case here, Grasmoor plays a reluctant second fiddle to its lesser neighbour, Eel Crag. Grasmoor is rather out on a limb, away from the centre of topographical happenings, the role of pivot being assumed by Eel Crag which exercises an influence and overview of the surrounding terrain, is the culmination of ascending ridges, determines the direction of flow of its streams and generally acts as a father figure to the lesser fells in its immediate vicinity. Grasmoor has no such

From Grasmoor 4: the two pools to Grasmoor

Map labels:
continuation WHITESIDE 4
continuation HOPEGILL HEAD 6
sheepfold
Gasgale Gill
Coledale Hause
BRAITHWAITE
Dove Crags
GRASMOOR ▲ 2791
continuation EEL CRAG 4 continued page 71
pools
EEL CRAG
continuation WANDOPE 4 continued page 78
N
Thirdgill Head Man
Rannerdale Beck
continuation WHITELESS PIKE 2
BUTTERMERE via WHITELESS PIKE
ONE MILE

attributes: it stands alone, aloof, of massive proportions but with no supporting ridges, no subservient satellites, no family of its own and no close friends, and is unable to give its streams a choice of direction. Its one great appeal lies in the magnificent panorama afforded by its superior height.

Grasmoor excels, however, in its presentation to the Buttermere road at its base of a tremendous west face which soars nearly half a mile into the sky as a towering pyramid of intimidating aspect. No other mountain in Lakeland has so impressive an appearance from a public road. Beyond the grassy verges the ground steepens dramatically, becoming near-vertical as it leaps upwards and then narrows to a rocky apex above a savage downfall of scree, rocks and crags in a petrified avalanche of mountain debris. The face is split asunder by two sinister gullies where rock-climbers find limited sport but for walkers is quite unassailable and out of bounds. One look is sufficient to deter any thought of ascent, and significantly there are no foot-tracks leading even initially towards the sudden upsurge directly in front. It is remarkable that, although Grasmoor is very conveniently positioned for direct ascent, being alongside a road with ample car parking spaces, the challenge goes unheeded, the aspect of the mountain on this side being too daunting and formidable even to contemplate.

Nor are the two flanks any more promising. The north side overlooking Gasgale Gill is equally steep with scree runs falling from a top barrier of cliffs and continuing with little respite to Dove Crags, the gradients easing only as Coledale Hause is approached. The other side, facing south-east over the deep cutting of Rannerdale Beck, is a waste of scree at a high angle and totally uninviting.

The boundaries of Grasmoor are clearly defined by Gasgale Gill and Rannerdale Beck, both watercourses destined for the River Cocker, the Rannerdale stream first passing through Crummock Water. To add to its demerits, Grasmoor has no tarns to show to visitors but they will be more than compensated by the superlative views of the Buttermere lakes it commands.

The best place for appraising a mountain is a point opposite at mid-height – rarely can its proportions be fully appreciated when viewed from a valley or from a summit of similar elevation. For this reason, the eastern edge of Mellbreak is a grandstand seat for a study of the western side of Grasmoor.

There are few weaknesses in the structure of Grasmoor

by which the summit may be attained and only one that permits an easy approach, the others being expensive in energy and physical discomfort. This west face must be ruled out entirely as impossibly steep and unsafe.

The name of the fell is commonly misspelt as Grassmoor, even in print, by writers who would never dream of misspelling Grasmere Grassmere. There is only one 's'. The *gras* derives from *grise* – wild boar – as in so many Lakeland names, e.g. Grisedale. Probably most visitors to Grasmoor will remember the fell for its extent and its luxurious carpet of mossy turf, close-cropped by the resident sheep who range these broad acres.

Many cairns adorn the ample top but the highest is not in doubt: it is a great heap of stones roughly shaped into compartments to serve as shelters from the wind. Nearby is a smaller windbreak of stones and, beyond, is the brink of the tremendous plunge of crags and scree on the west face, confirming the hopelessness of direct ascents on this side. It is a fearful sight better viewed from Grasmoor End which is reached by a short walk from the summit. There is a covering of small stones around the main cairn but this gives way to pleasant turf as the summit widens into a plateau eastwards.

Grasmoor's superior altitude gives it distinction as a viewpoint. The panorama from the summit cairn is uninterrupted and comprehensive, all the major heights in the district being revealed in a crowded horizon. The broad top, however, hides the surrounding valleys, the prospect being exclusively of distant mountain ranges. This deficiency, however, is remedied by a short walk to the edge of the west face where great depth is suddenly added to the scene, the prospect southwards being of classic quality and one of the finest in Lakeland. Grasmoor's other short-comings are forgiven when the summit is reached.

Having visited the summit of Grasmoor, the route re-traces its steps to the two pools. Just before reaching the pools, bear right onto a minor path that crosses over the path to Whiteless Pike and continues ahead. When the path fades, continue uphill in the same direction to the summit of **WANDOPE**.

There is no mountain not worth climbing, and any summit above the magic figure of 2500 feet might be expected to attract fellwalkers and peak-baggers in large numbers. To some extent, Wandope (2533 feet) does this, but only because the top almost gets in the way of a popular triangular tour based on Buttermere–Whiteless Pike, Eel Crag, Grasmoor – and the cairn is visited almost as a matter of course (if indeed it is noticed at all) and by the simplest of detours. Wandope is only well seen, in fact, from the uninhabited valley of Sail Beck from which it rises in a mile-long wall, rimmed a thousand feet above by a line of shattered crags. The hinterland of the summit is the upland prairie dominated by Eel Crag and Grasmoor, and it is along here that most walkers pass, often without realising that the insignificant swell of grass on the eastern fringe is distinguished both by a name and an altitude above the 2500 feet contour.

Wandope might be expected to stand out more conspicuously from the greater mass behind, for it is partly severed by two gills which drain from the plateau and immediately form, on either side, deeply carved rifts, one a scree-choked

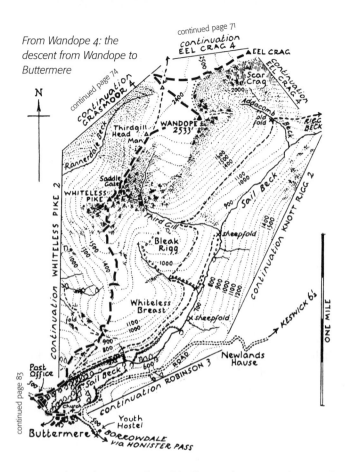

From Wandope 4: the descent from Wandope to Buttermere

continued page 71

continued page 74

continuation EEL CRAG 4

EEL CRAG

continuation EEL CRAG 4

continuation GRASMOOR 4

N

Rannerdale Beck

Thirdgill Head Man

WANDOPE 2533'

Scar Crag

Addacomb Beck

old fold

RIGG BECK

continuation KNOTT RIGG 2

Saddle Gate

WHITELESS PIKE

Third Gill

Sail Beck

continuation WHITELESS PIKE 2

Bleak Rigg

sheepfold

Whiteless Breast

fold

sheepfold

KESWICK 6½

ONE MILE

Post Office

Sail Beck

ROAD

Newlands Hause

continuation ROBINSON 3

continued page 85

Church

Buttermere

Youth Hostel

BORROWDALE via HONISTER PASS

ravine, the other a profound hollow. These are Third Gill and Addacomb Beck and both go down to Sail Beck. The first is a place to avoid, the second a place to visit or at least look at from the rim of its crater: the profound *cwm* is Adda-comb Hole, a perfect example of a hanging valley, quite the

78

finest in Lakeland, and a remarkable specimen of natural sculpturing. The issuing stream has a high waterfall and the whole scene is a complete geography lesson without words.

As for the fell's name, many generations of Lakeland walkers have known it as Wandope (Wandup a century ago). Now the Ordnance Survey claim good authority for naming it Wanlope and up-and-coming walkers in future will no doubt use this new spelling without question. But old-timers never will. [In fact, the OS has now reverted to Wandope on current maps.]

Apart from the view, the summit is unremarkable, being a smooth grassy parade, kept neat and trim by grazing sheep. The stones of the cairn, which stands near the brink of the great downfall to Sail Beck, were obviously not provided by the summit itself, and some anonymous enthusiast must, in days gone by, have laboured mightily in bringing them up from the escarpment.

Pride of place in the view must be conceded to the Scafells, from here looking magnificent, but scarcely less impressive is the scene eastwards, where range after range of tall fells cross the line of vision to culminate finally in the long Helvellyn skyline.

Many walkers must have been beguiled by the southern ridge of Wandope into the false assumption that if they follow it down, it will lead them to Whiteless Pike. Every step here, however, puts Whiteless Pike further out of reach while bringing it nearer, because of the rough ravine forming between. The southern pike is, in fact, a snare and a delusion. To gain the true one, aim west from the summit of Wandope and make for the cairn on Thirdgill Head Man. Go down a narrowing crest to

Saddle Gate for the climb to **WHITELESS PIKE**, *now directly ahead.*

The summit (2159 feet) is small and exposed, with an untidy accumulation of stones on the highest point. Except as a viewing station, it has little of interest, Like Causey Pike, its counterpart at the other extreme of the Eel Crag ridge, Whiteless Pike has a great advantage as a viewpoint by reason of the small uplifted summit and the abrupt downfall therefrom, which together permit a prospect both wide and deep, a view of valleys as well as of mountains. The Scafell mass is most excellently displayed and is nowhere better seen than from this northern side of Buttermere, the valley scene below the distant, lofty skyline being very beautiful; indeed, the whole rich picture is crowded with lovely detail.

Less rugged but not less charming is the appearance of Crummock Water and Loweswater to the west. In contrast, nearby Grasmoor and Wandope fill up the northern horizon rather unattractively.

From the summit of Whiteless Pike, the path down to Buttermere village is 1¾ miles on a good path, with superb views. Where the path forks at the level of a small wood, the left path should be taken.

[*See* page 65 for a description of Buttermere village.]

DAY SEVEN

Buttermere to Wasdale Head

There is no fairer scene in Lakeland than the charming valley of Buttermere, a delight at all times of the year and in any condition, its joys undiminished even by rain. Buttermere has a glorious surround of fells around the perimeter of the lake, most of them in a continuous line at a high level and not easy to define individually from the lovely shore paths.

The High Stile range, forming a mountainous barrier between the parallel valleys of Ennerdale and Buttermere, is one of the most beautiful of ridge walks. It is, moreover, free from complexities, rising on a straight north-west–south-east axis without deviations. Three summits overtop the general level of the ridge, High Stile being the central and highest, and High Crag and Red Pike, little lower in altitude, being sturdy supporters on each side. Both flanks are steeply scarped, High Stile and High Crag having precipitous crags on the Buttermere side, and there are conifer plantings along their bases although not extending high enough above Buttermere to mar the impressive grandeur of the scene. Red Pike is gentler and has a scattering of deciduous trees on its lower slopes. The range makes a tremendous background to the Buttermere valley and lake, this being the finest aspect, a picture of surpassing beauty even by Lakeland standards. The ascent from Buttermere reveals the grandest features of the range and excels in loveliness and charm: every step is a delight.

In the Lake District there are dozens of Raven Crags and Black Crags, many Dodds and several other instances of name-repetition in different areas. Amongst the major fells, there are two High Raises, two High Pikes and two Harter Fells – all fortunately well dispersed in widely separated localities. But two Red Pikes, only three miles apart, require distinct identification. It is usual to refer to this one as the Buttermere Red Pike, and the other, which is higher and bulkier, but for which the name is less suited, as the Wasdale Red Pike.

Syenite in the rock and subsoil of the fell produces the rich red colouring that has given this Red Pike its name and this is particularly marked in places where surface disturbance has occurred, remaining brilliant until weathering results in a more sombre ruddiness.

NOTE FOR THIS EDITION: In the original edition of this book, the route to Red Pike was via Far Ruddy Beck, with an alternative via Sour Milk Gill. In this edition, the latter route is preferred since the erosion mentioned by AW has now been superbly repaired.

From the village of Buttermere a path leaves the bridge near the outflow of the lake, and trends slightly left through Burtness Wood. The variation, climbing alongside Sour Milk Gill from its foot, is scarcely worth considering; the way up, amongst trees and boulders, is steep and rough. Above the wood, the path makes a wide loop to the left to ease the steepness before

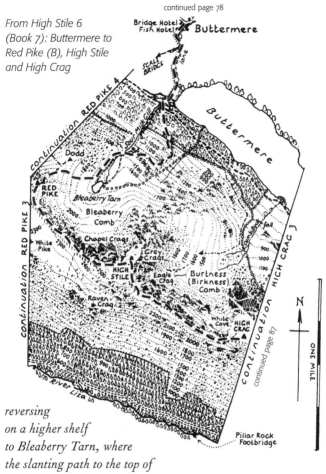

continued page 78

*From High Stile 6
(Book 7): Buttermere to
Red Pike (B), High Stile
and High Crag*

Bridge Hotel
Fish Hotel
Buttermere

SCALE BRIDGE

lane

Buttermere

continuation RED PIKE 4

Dodd

RED PIKE

Bleaberry Tarn

*Bleaberry
Comb*

continuation RED PIKE 3

White Pike

Chapel Crags

*Grey
Crags*

HIGH STILE

*Eagle
Crag*

*Burtness
(Birkness)
Comb*

fall

continuation HIGH CRAG 3

*Raven
Crag*

White
Cove

HIGH CRAG

continuation HIGH CRAG 2

continued page 87

N

ONE MILE

River Liza

Pillar Rock
Footbridge

*reversing
on a higher shelf
to Bleaberry Tarn, where
the slanting path to the top of*
RED PIKE *which I remember as a thin track, is now so wide and
obvious that only a genius could miss it.*

Red Pike's summit (2479 feet) projects from the main
mass of the fell boldly, like a promontory from a cliff-face,

having a steep fall on three sides, a flat top, and a gentle decline to a grassy plateau southwards, which is crossed by a boundary fence above the Ennerdale slope. The cairn, a big heap of stones, occupies the abrupt corner of the promontory directly at the head of the Buttermere path. The top is grassy, with an intermingling of small outcrops and stony patches. The view from Red Pike is notable for the number of lakes that can be seen, *really* seen and not merely glimpsed; their prominence adds an unusual beauty to the scene. Despite High Stile's impending bulk, the mountain view is quite satisfying; the Grasmoor group, seen from tip to toe, is very conspicuous.

Marker cairns head south to the old fence, which may be followed across excellent turf to the stony rise of High Stile, but in clear weather keep to the edge of the escarpment to get the best views.

There are impressive peeps down the gullies of Chapel Crags as the path rounds a comb. This is Bleaberry Comb, identified by the dark pool of Bleaberry Tarn on the floor of another hanging valley.

The Buttermere valley is robbed of winter sunshine by a rugged mountain wall exceeding 2000 feet in height and of unusual steepness, its serrated skyline seeming almost to threaten the green fields and dark lake and homesteads far below in its shadow. No mountain range in Lakeland is more impressive than this, no other more spectacularly sculptured, no other more worth climbing and exploring. Here the scenery assumes truly Alpine characteristics, yet without sacrifice of the intimate charms, the romantic atmosphere, found in Lakeland and nowhere else. The range is magnificently carved to a simple design on a massive scale.

Most mountains have a good side and a not-so-good side, and High Stile – along with Red Pike and High Crag – conforms to the rule. The Buttermere side of the ridge is tremendously exciting and darkly mysterious, compelling attention, but the other flank, by comparison, is plain and dull, without secrets, falling to the forests of Ennerdale steeply but lacking attractive adornment; for here the contours do not twist and leap about, they run evenly in straight lines.

The fringe of pines on the shore of Buttermere near Gatesgarth has formed a frame for many a photograph of the huge bastion of High Stile. This is one of several viewpoints associated with the early camera studies of the Abraham Brothers of Keswick, whose pictures were an introduction and inducement to Lakeland for many people and which, eighty years later, have never been surpassed for clarity of detail and atmosphere.

*Two cairns a few yards apart occupy a rocky eminence immediately above the abrupt fall of rocks northwards and are magnificent viewpoints and are usually considered to mark the highest point of **HIGH STILE** although this is disputed by the Ordnance Survey triangulation station indicated by a large cairn nearby.*

On a perfect summer's day, the summit of High Stile (2644 feet) is a place to linger: there is so much to see, such a feeling of well-being. The prospect from the summit, especially looking north, has the hallmark of excellence. If viewpoints were awarded Oscars, this would be a popular nomination.

Across the gulf of Ennerdale, Great Gable and the Scafells are prominent and Pillar is directly opposite, its famous Rock seen frontally and its declining western ridge and foothills terminated by the full length of Ennerdale Water. More distantly, the Helvellyn and Skiddaw ranges are seen overtopping others. But the gem of the view, the scene that captivates by its colour and beauty, and by the depth of vision, is the perfect setting of the Buttermere valley in lovely surroundings far below and a resplendent Crummock Water encompassed by lofty heights. Rising steeply out of the valley and seen from tip to toe in comprehensive detail are the north-western fells, posing proudly as though for a family photograph: a view ranking amongst the best in Lakeland.

*Leaving the summit of High Stile, the next objective is High Crag one mile away. There is no path at first but one forms when the ridge narrows. The line of fence posts is continuous to **HIGH CRAG**, and it is important to keep them in sight in bad weather. Looking back to High Stile from the ridge, a view of Eagle Crag in profile, and Grey Crags, more distant across the depths of Burtness Comb, is seen.*

Burtness Comb has no tarn and cannot compete with Bleaberry Comb in popular favour. Yet it is the finer of the two, as cragsmen have long realised, and is a grand place to spend a quiet day. Unlike most mountain hollows, its floor is bone-dry and even the beck is partly subterranean; it is notable for a rich July harvest of bilberries which grow in lush carpets among the tumbled boulders.

High Crag is the least known of the three linked peaks of the High Stile range towering above the Buttermere valley

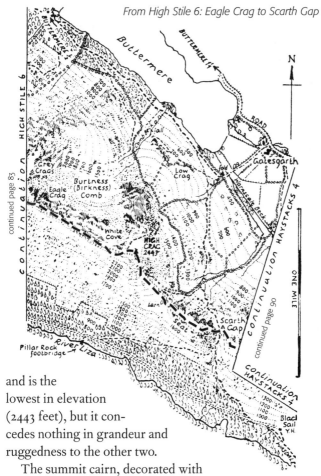

continued page 83

continuation HIGH STILE 6

continuation HAYSTACKS 4

continued page 90

continuation HAYSTACKS 4

N

Buttermere

Buttermere

Buttermerelt

ROAD

Gatesgarth

ONE MILE

Grey Crags

Eagle Crag

Burtness (Birkness) Comb

Low Crag

White Cove

HIGH CRAG 2443

Scarth Gap

Pillar Rock footbridge

River Liza

Black Sail Y.H.

and is the lowest in elevation (2443 feet), but it concedes nothing in grandeur and ruggedness to the other two.

The summit cairn, decorated with discarded iron fence posts, stands on the extreme eastern edge of the ridge and commands uninterrupted views in that direction, the finest aspect being of the head of

Ennerdale backed by Great Gable and Kirk Fell, the latter overtopped by the Scafell group. Nearer and below eye level are Scarth Gap and Haystacks, the next objectives; the extensive panorama culminates in the distant skyline of the Helvellyn range.

High Crag's formidable northern buttress is the finest object in the High Stile range. Eastwards are vast scree runs, where few men venture; the continuation of the ridge on this side is at first unpleasantly stony until an easier slope of grass leads down to a depression beyond which the ridge re-asserts itself as a distinctive crest and then falls abruptly in crags and scree to the top of the Scarth Gap Pass.

Scarth Gap, at one time more often spelt Scarf Gap, carries a popular path between Buttermere and the head of Ennerdale at Black Sail, so popular in fact that it has needed repair against erosion.

*The top of the pass is marked by a large cairn and near this point our ridge path from High Crag to Haystacks crosses. From Scarth Gap a steep and much corroded path turns left to the summit of **HAYSTACKS**, passing a charming rocky pool on the way.*

This final path has suffered severely from the tread of boots, so much so that wardens have fashioned rough steps to contain the traffic. This I deplore. Steps are for going upstairs, not for climbing mountains. Erosion of paths is a growing problem and the remedy is to educate people to walk circumspectly and in single file, keeping strictly to the path and not trampling the verges. It is wrong to castigate the guidebook writers.

Dear Haystacks! Here is a rugged height, little in stature

and small in extent, encircled by much loftier fells, some of international renown, yet standing quite unabashed by their greater presence in the landscape and not acknowledging inferiority to any of them. Like a shaggy and undisciplined terrier in the midst of a company of sleek foxhounds, Haystacks looks irascible, defiantly aggressive, and a bad-tempered little monster, not caring a damn for anybody or anything, and if blessed with lungs would probably demand attention by yapping and barking all day long. It is unusual in structure, not conforming to any pattern and stoutly asserting its right to be called a mountain despite a lack of height, a superior mountain because it is certainly not prepared to concede that any of its neighbours, not even Great Gable and Pillar, which look down at it, are more imposing or important.

Some misinformed sources have defined a mountain as a hill which exceeds 2000 feet in height. Of course they are wrong. The status of mountain is not determined by any arbitrary level of altitude but by appearance. Rocks and ruggedness, roughness of terrain and a commanding presence are the essential qualifications. I prefer the definition in my old dictionary: 'a large mass of earth and rock rising above the adjacent land'. Those who say that Haystacks is not a mountain because it does not top 2000 feet should go and see it. Or better still, climb it; Haystacks would be mortally offended if classed merely as a hill. Everything expected of a mountain is here: rocks, crags, bogs, runnels of water, tarns, boulders, scree and glorious views.

So why does Haystacks win the affection of all walkers? You have to climb to the top and wander about to under-

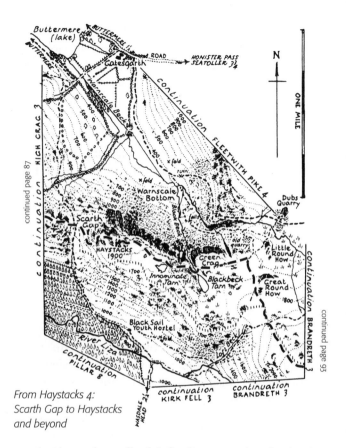

From Haystacks 4: Scarth Gap to Haystacks and beyond

Within the map:
Buttermere (lake)
ROAD
Gatesgarth
HONISTER PASS SEATOLLER 7½
N
ONE MILE
continuation HIGH CRAG 3
continued page 87
continuation FLEETWITH PIKE 4
Warnscale Bottom
Dubs Quarry
Scarth Gap
old quarry
HAYSTACKS 1900'
Green Crag
Little Round How
continuation BRANDRETH 3
Innominate Tarn
Blackbeck Tarn
Great Round How
Black Sail Youth Hostel
continued page 93
River Liza
continuation PILLAR 8
continuation KIRK FELL 3
continuation BRANDRETH 3
WASDALE HEAD 2½

stand. Above the wall of defending crags is a fascinating landscape, a confusing labyrinth of miniature peaks and tors, of serpentine tracks in rampant heather, of lovely tarns and tarnlets, of crags and screes, of marshes and streams, of rocks for climbing and rocks not for climbing, of surprises around every corner, with magnificent views all around.

90

Adrenalin runs fast in this natural wonderland. For a man trying to forget a persistent worry, the top of Haystacks is a complete cure.

Haystacks is absolutely right in demanding special attention, although perhaps exaggerating in claiming a degree of superiority over all other fells in the district. To say that there are few to match it would be a fairer assessment of relative merits. If mountains had fan clubs, Haystacks would have a legion of members. And I would be the first to enrol.

The spelling of Haystacks as one word is a personal preference of the author (and others) and probably arises from a belief that the name originated from the resemblance of the scattered tors on the summit to stacks of hay in a field. If this were so, the one word *Haystacks* would be correct (as it is in *Haycock*). But learned authorities state that the name derives from the Icelandic 'stack' meaning a 'columnar rock' and that the true interpretation is *High Rocks*.

The highest part of the fell is a small rocky ridge, fifty yards in length, with a cairn at each end and a tarn alongside to the west. The two cairns are at approximately the same elevation, but the north one, lying on the line of the path across the top of the fell, is usually reckoned to be the true summit. The actual height has not been definitely determined, but is often quoted as 1750 feet. This does Haystacks much less than justice, and 1900 feet is my own estimate. [The latest Ordnance Survey map allots 1959 feet to Haystacks.] Haystacks fails to qualify for inclusion in the author's 'best half-dozen' only because of inferior height, a deficiency in vertical measurement. Another thousand feet would have made all the difference.

But for beauty, variety and interesting detail, for sheer fascination and unique individuality, the summit-area of Haystacks is supreme. This is in fact the best fell-top of all – a place of great charm and fairyland attractiveness. Seen from a distance, these qualities are not suspected: indeed, on the contrary, the appearance of Haystacks is almost repellent when viewed from the higher surrounding peaks: black are its bones and black is its flesh. With its thick covering of heather it is dark and sombre even when the sun sparkles the waters of its many tarns, gloomy and mysterious even under a blue sky. There are fierce crags and rough screes and outcrops that will be grittier still when the author's ashes are scattered here.

Yet the combination of features, of tarn and tor, of cliff and cove, the labyrinth of corners and recesses, the maze of old sheepwalks and paths, form a design, or a lack of design, of singular appeal and absorbing interest. One can forget even a raging toothache on Haystacks.

Because of its low elevation, views from Haystacks are restricted by the ring of higher peaks all around and only to the north and east are distant horizons glimpsed, formed by Skiddaw and the Helvellyn range; otherwise the prospect from the summit is severely circumscribed. Nearby, and seen in intimate detail, are Great Gable, Pillar, High Crag, Grasmoor, Robinson and Dale Head, all looking down patronisingly at the shaggy little mountain in their midst. The gem of the view is the Buttermere valley and its lakes. The best places to view from are the edge of the northern cliffs or from the top of the great cleft containing the outflow of Blackbeck Tarn.

The path off Haystacks, by way of Innominate and Black-beck Tarns, passes through the finest scenery. The type of path that has most appeal to fellwalkers is the in-and-out up-and-down variety that discloses a variety of new and surprising vistas. One of the best of these is the traverse from Haystacks to Green Crag, which additionally has the merit of threading a way through impressive rock scenery.

Green Crag presents to the vast hollow of Warnscale a steep and rocky front to which a few trees cling, but on

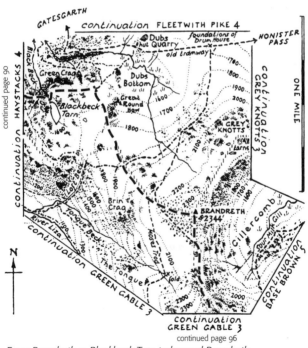

continued page 96

From Brandreth 3: Blackbeck Tarn to beyond Brandreth

other sides is gently inclined to a rounded summit. It is severed from Haystacks, of which it is properly a part, by the formidable ravine of Black Beck.

Innominate Tarn, a jewel in the crown of Haystacks, is a lovely sheet of water in a hollow enclosed by heathery undulations and watched over by Great Gable and Pillar. It derives its name from the fact of not having one. It was formerly considered to be nameless, although old Ordnance maps indicate it as Loaf Tarn, a title happily forgotten, and not good enough for so lovely a gem.

*The indefinite junction of the Brandreth path below Great Round How should be watched for carefully – it occurs just before the main path swings left and starts to descend towards Dubs Quarry. From the corner of the fence (posts only) there is no cause for further deviation, the fence leading directly to the summit of **BRANDRETH** up an easy grass slope and crossing two well-known paths in the course of doing so.*

Brandreth is an intermediate height (2344 feet) on the broad tilted ridge, almost a tableland, rising gently from the back of Honister Crag and culminating in Great Gable. Its summit is little higher than the general level of the plateau and has nothing of particular interest; indeed, the path along the ridge takes a wide sweep to avoid it, preferring to maintain an easy contour rather than go up and down over the top.

Brandreth's one claim to distinction is based on its superb view of the High Stile range flanked by the valleys of Ennerdale and Buttermere, a magnificent prospect; but this is a view as well seen from the west slope, around which the path curves, as from the top.

This western slope is broad and sprawling, part of it

declining to Ennerdale and part reshaping into the undulating summit of Haystacks; in sharp contrast, the eastern is abruptly cut away in cliffs falling into the great upland basin of Gillercomb.

Brandreth's position on the Derwent–Cocker–Liza watershed is sufficient guarantee of a commanding view, and this is extensive in all directions except south where the two Gables form a near and lofty horizon. Best of all the objects in view are the Grasmoor fells in the north-west, soaring in splendid array from deeply inurned Crummock Water. Pillar and High Stile are also well displayed.

For photographic purposes, note that the beautiful view north-west is seen to greater advantage from the western slope below the summit. In fine weather, a stroll down by the west fence might well produce the most magnificent picture of the year. Contrast and composition are excellent. Buttermere will not actually be seen from the top cairn by anyone less than 7 feet tall, but a few paces north-west will bring it into view. Go just a bit further, 60 yards, for a sight of Innominate Tarn.

Follow the fence south to join the Honister–Great Gable path again which is distinct and well cairned on the long climb to the top of **GREEN GABLE**.

A thousand people or more reach the summit cairn of Green Gable every year, yet it is probably true to say that no visitor to Lakeland ever announced at breakfast that this fell was his day's objective; and, if he did, his listeners would assume a slip of the tongue: of course, he must mean Great Gable. The two Gables are joined like Siamese twins, but they are not likenesses of each other. Great Gable is the

continued page 93

continued page 100

*From Green Gable 3: to beyond
Green Gable*

mighty
mountain
that every
walker wants to
climb; Green Gable
is a stepping stone to it
but otherwise of no account.
All eyes are fixed on Great
Gable; Green Gable is
merely something met *en
route.* So think most folk who pass from one to the other.

But Green Gable is not at all insignificant. At 2603 feet,
its altitude, by Lakeland standards, is considerable. A sharp
peaked summit, more delicately wrought than Great
Gable's, adds distinction. Rock-climbers' crags adorn its
western fringe. Important paths reach it on all sides.
Unsought though the top may be, nevertheless it is much
used and well known through the accident of its position.

It is a crowning misfortune for Green Gable, however,
that the volcanic upheaval ages ago stopped upheaving at a
moment when this fell was in a position completely subservient to a massive neighbour, and so fashioned the summit that it is forever destined to look up into the pillared

crags of Great Gable as a suppliant before a temple. It is because of the inferiority induced by Big Brother that Green Gable cannot ever expect to be recognised as a fine mountain in its own right.

Green Gable is not really an appropriate name for the fell. Grass covers the lower and mid slopes only, the higher reaches being an arid, colourless waste of stones completely unrelieved by areas of vegetation.

It is a pity that most visitors to the summit are in a hurry to get off it, for the narrow strip of rough ground between the cairn and the rim of the western crags is a fine perch to study the massive architecture of Great Gable and the deep pit of stones below it: this is a tremendous scene.

It might almost be thought that the summit had been expressly constructed for observing the northern crags of Great Gable, so convenient a platform is it for this purpose. The scene calls for first attention; wander west a few yards from the cairn (not too many!) to appreciate the full proportions of the cliff above Stone Cove. Elsewhere the view is very comprehensive, little of the district being hidden by Great Gable. The best picture, a beautiful one, is north-west, where four sheets of water nestle in the folds of rugged and colourful mountains: note how Blackbeck Tarn appears to spill into Buttermere although in fact there is an unseen mile between them.

From the summit of Green Gable, Great Gable is only a stone's throw away, a massive object with the black cliffs of Gable Crag prominent. A five-minute descent leads to the col of Windy Gap which is the narrow col linking the two mountains. It is rarely used as a pass, and is in fact only of use as such for travellers coming from the east by Sprinkling Tarn and seeking a direct course for Ennerdale or Buttermere, or vice versa. Windy Gap is crossed to a path skirting the cliffs.

This climbs to the left of Gable Crag: a well-blazed trail with a large population on a fine day. In the final stages, it is worth making a short detour to the edge of Gable Crag for the sensational views therefrom down into Stone Cove.

The rocky passage then leads on to the top of **GREAT GABLE** *(2949 feet).*

Great Gable is everybody's favourite. The very name is a compelling magnet, the aspect of the mountain on all sides is challenging and its ascent a highlight in the itineraries of all active walkers in Lakeland. Great Gable caters for all sorts: youngsters find an exuberant delight in clambering to the top, novices serving their apprenticeship on the fells gain valuable experience, seasoned walkers often return to resume an intimate acquaintance, and intrepid rock-climbers aim for familiar crags in eager anticipation of exhilarating hours in their awesome and austere company.

The mountain is simple in structure, without complications, matching the popular concept of a mountain form: a steep-sided pyramid tapering to a slender top. Gable is all ups and downs, a huge cone of severe and uncompromising gradients with no halts in the steepness, no tracts of flat ground to relieve ascent or descent.

It was the early dalesfolk of Wasdale Head who gave the mountain its apt name and they could not have chosen a more appropriate one for the imposing presence that closes and dominates their valley. Its finest aspect is from Wasdale Head, seen as a strong yet graceful tower with a summit defended by crags. From Lingmell Beck at its base, relentless slopes soar upwards for half a mile in a lateral distance of less than a mile, under a covering of stones and boulders and rock debris so extensive that the cliffs from which they fell in ages past must have been of far greater proportions than the remnants that remain today as the Great Napes. These slopes are an untrodden wasteland of scree at a high angle, an uninviting and arid desert.

On the north side, too, the shadowed precipice of Gable Crag has shed fans of scree into the desolate gathering grounds of the River Liza. The east flank is more accommodating and it is on this side that walkers are offered a route of ascent that is the least arduous and has welcome vestiges of greenery amongst the stones. Direct approaches from the west are ruled out by further interminable slopes of scree. Seldom does a day pass without visitors appearing on the summit yet, despite the popularity of the climb, walkers are severely constrained by the rugged texture of the ground, there being little incentive to stray from the few paths. Great Gable has not been tamed and never will be.

The failing of Great Gable is that it holds few mysteries, all its wares being openly displayed. The explorer, the man who likes to look around corners and discover secrets and intimacies, may be disappointed, not on a first visit, which cannot fail to be interesting, but on subsequent occasions. There are no cavernous recesses, no hidden tarns, no combes, no hanging valleys, no waterfalls, no streams other than those forming the boundaries. Yet walkers tread its familiar tracks again and again, almost as a ritual, and climbers queue to scale its familiar rocks. The truth is,

Great Gable casts a spell. It starts as an honourable adversary and becomes a friend.

Great Gable is the centre of an area of 3000 acres of high fells acquired by the Fell and Rock Climbing Club as a memorial to the members who lost their lives in the 1914–18 war, and was given to the National Trust in 1923. In June 1924 a dedicatory tablet, affixed to the summit rocks, was unveiled at a moving ceremony in the presence of a gathering of five hundred fellow members and friends. Since then, it has been the inspiring scene of an annual Remembrance Service in November. It is a fitting place to pay homage to men who

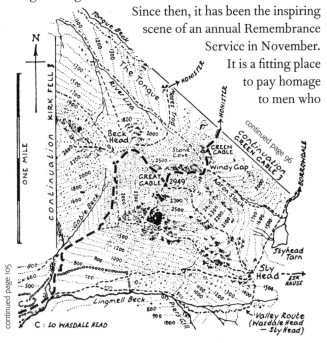

From Great Gable 6: Green Gable to Great Gable and the descent to Wasdale

once loved to walk on these hills and gave their lives defending the right of others to enjoy the same happy freedom, for the ultimate crest of Gable is truly characteristic of the best of mountain Lakeland: a rugged crown of rock and boulders in chaotic profusion, a desert without life, a harsh and desolate peak thrust high in the sky above the profound depths all around.

Gable, tough and strong all through its height, has here made a final gesture by providing an outcrop of rock even in its last inches, so that one must climb to touch the cairn (which, being hallowed as a shrine by fellwalkers everywhere, let no man tear asunder lest a thousand curses accompany his guilty flight!).

There are few days in the year when no visitor arrives on the summit. Snow and ice and severe gales may defy those who aspire to reach it in winter, but in the summer months there is a constant parade of perspiring pedestrians across the top from early morning to late evening. To many fellwalkers this untidy bit of ground is Mecca.

Great Gable's summit is rather special to me for a particular reason. In 1967, it came as a great surprise to me when I was awarded the MBE in recognition of the completion of my *Pictorial Guides to the Lakeland Fells*, which I had compiled between 1952 and 1966. It wasn't until 1980 that I learned from a correspondent that, fourteen years earlier, a fellwalker from Southport had spent the day on the summit of Great Gable collecting signatures to a petition which was later sent to Downing Street.

An excellent panorama, rich in detail and extending to all points of the compass, rewards those who reach the summit.

The view is predominantly of mountains and fells arranged in a distant circle, all the principal heights in the district being seen except the Coniston fells which are hidden by the Scafell range. Sprinkling Tarn and a few others are glimpsed, Wastwater is the only lake in sight. The radiating valleys of Eskdale, Wasdale, Ennerdale, Buttermere and Borrowdale carve their way through the high ground, adding a touch of greenery to a sombre picture.

The summit plateau should not be left without first taking a short stroll of 120 yards south-west in the direction of Wasdale to the Westmorland Cairn standing on the edge of a downfall of crags.

Erected in 1876 by two brothers of the name of Westmorland to mark what they considered to be the finest mountain viewpoint in the district, this solidly built and tidy cairn is well known to climbers and walkers alike, and has always been respected. The cairn has maintained its original form throughout the years quite remarkably: apart from visitors who like to add a pebble, it has suffered neither from the weather nor from human despoilers. It stands on the extreme brink of the south face, above steep crags, and there is an arresting view of Wasdale Head, a patchwork of small fields half a mile below, and of Wastwater in the distance beyond. There is also to be seen from this point the massive build-up of the Scafells from valley level to the skyline ridge. Nearby, below the cairn, the upper rocks of the Napes appear as a serrated fringe in front of a profound void.

Rocky platforms around make the place ideal for a halt after climbing Great Gable.

*

NOTE FOR THIS EDITION: This section of the walk was the first half of AW's Day Four. In this edition, it is Day Seven and ends by descending from Great Gable to Wasdale Head via Beck Head. Do not attempt to descend to the valley bottom direct from the Westmorland Cairn.

Return to the summit of Great Gable and pick a way carefully down the north-west ridge, avoiding false trails that lead only to boulder slopes and keeping generally near the angle of the ridge where the footing is firmest. The descent to Beck Head is now marked by a line of cairns. When an intermittent line of fence posts is joined, the remainder of the route is assured, the posts leading across the depression of Beck Head.

On the descent to Beck Head, a view opens up ahead of the long afforested valley of Ennerdale but attention will be focused on the pround presence of Pillar, its long and serrated eastern edge defined by shadow, and sharp eyes will note Pillar Rock in silhouette on the Ennerdale flank.

The depression of Beck Head with its small pools is the turning point for the end of Day Seven. The path – known as Moses' Trod after a colourful Lakeland character, a quarryman from Honister – now contours the west slope of Great Gable to reach Gavel Neese. Here an upstanding rock still bears the name of Moses' Finger. Finally, there is an easy and pleasant descent to Wasdale Head (see map on page 105 for continuation of descent).

Those doing the Memorial Walk in its entirety will be able to make Wasdale Head their base for the next two nights; see pages 119–20 and 121 for descriptions of Wasdale Head.

The Wasdale Head Circuit

NOTE FOR THIS EDITION: Those walkers who stayed overnight at Wasdale Head, undertaking the walk in its entirety, should now return to Beck Head by the same route as the previous day's route.

A short lane leads from the inn at Wasdale Head to the cultivated fields of Burnthwaite from where the path ascending to Great Gable starts. The approach is pleasant, with the line of ascent in full view: a green and verdant carpet unfolds along the rising ridge, and ahead there is a promise of great interest to come. At 1500 feet, a track (Moses' Trod) escapes left to Beck Head.

From Beck Head, the route passes up the steep facing slope of Rib End, and visits first the lower and then the top summit of **KIRK FELL** *across a wide grassy plateau.*

Kirk Fell is the patron fell of Wasdale Head, a distinction little recognised. To most visitors in this grandest of all daleheads, Great Gable so catches the eye that Kirk Fell, next to it, is hardly looked at; and even the two other fells enclosing the valley, Lingmell and Yewbarrow, win more glances. Kirk Fell, although bulking large in the scene, is in fact plain and unattractive, a vast wall of bracken and grass, every yard of it much like the rest. Everybody's camera points to Great

Gable, nobody's to Kirk Fell. But look at the map. The streams coming down each side are long in meeting: for a mile or so at valley level they enclose a flat tongue of land at the foot of Kirk Fell. Every building in the little hamlet of

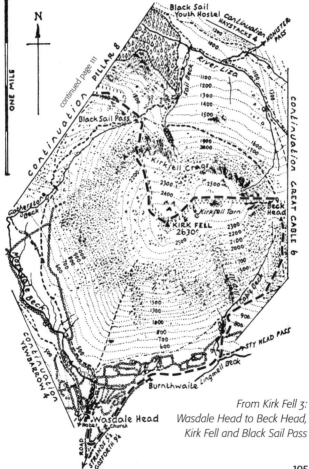

continued page 111
continuation PILLAR 8
continuation HAYSTACKS & HONISTER PASS
continuation GREAT GABLE 6
continuation YEWBARROW 4

From Kirk Fell 3:
Wasdale Head to Beck Head,
Kirk Fell and Black Sail Pass

Wasdale Head – cottages, farmhouses, church and hotel and all the valley pastures – lie in the map of Kirk Fell on this flat extension between the two streams. The fell takes its name from the church. Kirk Fell accommodates the community of Wasdale Head, but the footings in the valley of Great Gable and Lingmell and Yewbarrow are barren.

Bland the southern aspect may be, but the dark north face is very different. Here, shadowed cliffs seam the upper slopes in a long escarpment, a playground for climbers, above rock declivities that go down to the Liza in Ennerdale. Linking with Great Gable is the depression of Beck Head to the east; westwards is a counterpart in Black Sail Pass, linking with Pillar. And between is a broad undulating top, with tarns, the ruins of a wire fence, and twin summits: on the whole, a rather disappointing ornamentation, a poor crown for so massive a plinth.

Kirk Fell has two separate tops, the higher being at the head of the Wasdale slope in an area of stones. Here is the main cairn, which is combined with a wind shelter. The fence which otherwise follows the watershed strictly, rather oddly does not quite visit the highest point at 2630 feet. The other top, north-east, is appreciably lower, the cairn here surmounting a rocky outcrop. In a hollow between the two summits are two unattractive tarns, named as one, Kirkfell Tarn.

Great Gable dominates the scene but does not rob the view of detail, which is well distributed over all sectors. The Scafells look magnificent, and Criffel appears over High Crag.

Very easy walking by the fence leads to a steepening slope, and here a track materialises amongst the stones. When crags are reached, the fence does a bit of rock-climbing. Kirkfell Crags occur in two series, the first overlooking Black Sail Pass in a broken cliff and the other, steeply buttressing the north-east summit and exhibiting cleaner rock faces, having the adopted name of Boat How Crags. Keep the track underfoot, however, and after one awkward step, Black Sail Pass will be duly reached.

The pass is the climax of the route which crosses from Wasdale Head via the valley of Mosedale to Ennerdale.

When I was a young man and still living in Blackburn, my visits to the Lake District were of necessity restricted to day excursions on the train to Windermere and, in due course, I became very familiar with the glorious countryside within a ten-mile radius of the railway station. I longed to be able to get further afield. Studying the Ordnance Survey map of the district was a daily ritual for me over many years: I knew the details by heart although most of the region remained out of reach. I pinpointed all the mountains on the map, these having an exciting attraction for me: we had valleys and hills at home but no mountains. In particular, two mountain names fired my imagination: in the western fells were Pillar and Steeple, and for twenty years they plagued my mind until I was able to see and set foot on them. Even when I moved to Kendal, thereby bringing all the mountains within closer range, wartime restrictions on travel kept me in exile.

At last the chance came for a visit to Pillar and I set forth eagerly to realise a long ambition and see the promised pinnacles.

They were disappointing. Pillar was nothing like a pillar

and Steeple bore only a slight resemblance to a steeple. But the area of which they formed part was a revelation, an assembly of bare rocky peaks in a wilderness landscape very different from the lush greenery of the environs of Windermere: here was loneliness and solitude and an array of silent but challenging mountains. Pillar and Steeple had not the expected needle-sharp spires but they were wonderful members of a wonderful company.

I had known in advance that Pillar took its name from a famous rock on the Ennerdale side of the mountain: in fact, I was so steeped in the publications of the Fell and Rock Climbing Club and the excellent photographs of the Abraham brothers that I had long formed a mental picture of Pillar Rock in detail.

One of my evergreen memories is of that February day fifty years ago when I first visited Pillar. I climbed straight up from Ennerdale, which at that time had not been planted with conifers and was bare and desolate. I had not gone far when I was enveloped in a clammy mist, visibility being reduced to a few yards only. I had hoped to see Pillar Rock, having been thrilled by graphic reports of rock-climbing adventures on this wonderful monolith, but the blanket of mist blotted out everything except a few yards of ground around me. This flank of Pillar is one of the roughest in the district, a succession of craggy outcrops, and upward progress was laborious. Robbed of sight I struggled ever upwards, mercifully without meeting any insuperable obstacle. The mist did not relent, even for a moment, and the silence was profound: this was not a day for larks to be flying and singing. I did not bump into Pillar Rock and saw no sign of it. I began to sense that I was well off-course, this being confirmed when at long last I entered a scree gully that led me to the skyline of the west ridge some distance from the summit. I had spent four hours struggling up the rugged fellside like a blind man, seeing nothing beyond my grasp. I do not recall a mist as dense and immovable as this ...

The incident would not be worth the telling but for a remarkable transformation that occurred as I walked up to the summit. All at once, with a suddenness that transfixed me, I stepped out of the wet mist into brilliant and dazzling sunlight and above was a cloudless blue sky. I went up to the summit, now starkly clear. It was a walk in space. Just below me was the mist, stretching into the far distance but now having a ceiling and being no longer grey but a pure white. Clearly defined on this vaporous curtain was the shadow of a man. It was my shadow, walking when I walked, stopping when I stopped: the first time I had witnessed such a phenomenon. I spent a few minutes waving to the man in the mist, always getting a simultaneous response and then, as I went on down the east ridge, there was a gradual movement in the mist, then a swirling and boiling of the vapours followed by a swift dispersal and disappearance.

Very soon the mist vanished to disclose the valley below and the fells beyond. The rest of the day, as I went down to Wasdale Head and over to Eskdale, was gloriously sunny and warm.

The main ridge from Black Sail Pass to the summit is a pleasant walk without difficulty, three stony rises being succeeded by splendid turf. The east ridge is reached at Looking

Map labels visible:
ONE MILE

Ennerdale

SCARTH GAP

N

continuation SCOAT FELL

High Beck

White Pike
Pillar Rock

PILLAR
2927

Windgap Cove

Wind Gap

Wind Cove

continuation SCOAT FELL

continued page 115

Mosedale Beck

continuation RED PIKE (W)

From Pillar 7–8:
Black Sail Pass to Pillar
and Wind Gap

continued opposite

Stead and is followed up
alongside the remains of a
wire fence to the flat top of **PILLAR**.

[In his original itinerary, AW achieved the
summit of Pillar by the route described above,
and then made a detour to Pillar Rock from the
summit. In later writings, AW praised the High Level
Traverse approach to the summit of Pillar.

This branches from the east ridge at the foot of the first rise
beyond Looking Stead. The instant revelation comes upon top-
ping a small eminence crowned by Robinson's Cairn. From
here, a short foray up the stony fellside leads to a rising shelf,
the Shamrock Traverse, that gives an easy passage above the
Shamrock and comes face to face with High Man at close range.

SCARTH GAP
BUTTERMERE →

River Liza

1200
1100
1000

Black Sail
Youth Hostel

1000

Green Cove

Looking Stead

Crag

1900

1000

2100
2000

Black Sail Pass

1800

1600

Gatherstone Beck

1400
1200
1000
900
800
700

1000
1100
1200
1300
1400

KIRK FELL 3

CONTINUATION 2200 continued page 105

*A rough and loose track leaves excite-
ment behind and ascends the fellside
above the Rock to the summit of the
mountain. The High Level Route is
not only the royal road to Pillar
Rock but to Pillar mountain also.]
For the detour to Pillar Rock
from the top of Pillar,
leave the summit at
the north wind-
shelter. Pillar Rock
comes into view at
once, and a rough
loose track slithers
down to the point
where the first of its
buttresses (Pisgah) rises
from the fellside.*
Pillar Rock has been
likened to a shattered cathed-
ral but the simile is not only as
regards its imposing structure: the
Rock is twice the height of most cathe-
drals and far from being shattered is very
firmly rooted in the fellside. This is no crumbling edifice but an immense tower of solid and
immovable rock, nature's architecture on a massive scale
and constructed to a master design.

In essence, Pillar Rock is one tower superimposed on
another. From the base, a sheer wall soars upwards almost

vertically for 400 feet to halt for a breather at a commodious ledge bearing a cairn; this section is known as Low Man. Then after this brief respite the wall resumes its upward flight to come to rest finally on the top of the Rock, and the upper super-structure is called the High Man. The Rock is cut away from the fellside at High Man by a deep cleft and on both sides is severed from adjoining ground by gullies: thus it is a separate entity within clearly defined boundaries. Seen from the east, however, its isolation is not apparent since the dividing gully is hidden by a flanking cliff that seems to be part of the main mass; because of this deception, it has the name of Shamrock.

After a century and a half of exploration, Pillar Rock has yielded to the rock-climbing fraternity a wide variety of routes of ascent of all degrees of difficulty, those on the north front of Low Man and the west side of High Man in particular being of exceptional severity. To a non-climbing observer whose feet are firmly planted on easy ground nearby, the human flies inching their way up the precipitous walls of rock seem to be performing the impossible. Pillar Rock is for very brave men only.

Back on the summit of Pillar (2927 feet) all the interest is centred on the Ennerdale side, the summit being a flat and stony expanse lacking natural features and depending on man's creations to relieve the monotony of the scene. A cairn, an Ordnance column and two windshelters testify to the esteem in which Pillar is regarded by fellwalkers and the makers of maps. There is no awareness of imminent declivities all around, these being revealed only by a perambulation of the top. The distant view across the rather dull summit is magnificent in all directions. Great Gable and the entire Scafell range are seen to perfection, the northern fells and the Helvellyn group fill the horizon in great detail, and over the gulf of Windgap Cove an arresting skyline is formed by Scoat Fell, Steeple and the heights beyond as they decline to Ennerdale Water and the sea.

From the north windshelter, there is a sensational view down into Ennerdale with the High Man of Pillar Rock thrusting out of the steep fellside directly below.

From the summit of Pillar comes a rough descent south-west to the narrow col of Wind Gap neatly dividing Mosedale and Ennerdale and carrying a path between the two valleys.

The Ennerdale side is a scene of wild desolation with a ring of crags surrounding the lonely hollow of Windgap Cove. Although not classed as a pass in guide-books and not often used as such, the sharp col at the top of Windgap Cove between Pillar and Scoat Fell has all the characteristics of a true pass and, indeed, is one of the best defined in Lakeland. The situation of the col is exceedingly grand; like an eyrie, the col overlooks a savage untamed landscape of crags and rivers of scree where solitude is absolute and silence unbroken.

Across the col, there is a sharp rise to the top of Black Crag, the path then levelling to give easy progress to grass above the crag which falls precipitously into Windgap Cove. From the edge of the cliffs, a striking view is obtained of the slender pinnacle of Steeple, here seen springing high out of gloomy depths, its lofty and delicate proportions justifying its name.

The gulf between, bounded by the crags of Scoat Fell, is

the grim recess of Mirk Cove, an area of devastation uninviting and repelling.

After leaving Black Crag, the next objective is the summit of **SCOAT FELL** *(2760 feet), reached by an easy uphill trudge made more interesting by keeping to the edge overlooking Mirk Cove. The naming of mountain hollows as coves is uncommon in Lakeland, occurring only along this Ennerdale flank and in the Helvellyn range.*

Although often climbed from Wasdale as a part of the Mosedale Horseshoe, Scoat Fell has no fan club and few devotees, for the long plateau forming the top compares unfavourably with the more shapely summits of other fells even easier of access from Wasdale Head. Yet Scoat Fell triumphs over its disabilities and provides magnificent mountain scenery on all sides. The mile-long escarpment facing Ennerdale, between Wind Gap and Mirklin Cove, is tremendously exciting, wild and desolate terrain, interrupted only by a thin arête linking with Steeple, a subsidiary pinnacle of remarkable proportions towering gracefully across the void.

In the literature of the district, some writers have loosely referred to Scoat Fell as Steeple. While it must be conceded that Scoat Fell and Steeple are strictly one fell, the name Steeple clearly refers only to the sharp prominence to the north of the main summit. One has only to see it to realise this.

Walkers who insist on summit cairns being sited precisely on the highest part of a summit have suffered a frustration here, for the exact spot representing the maximum altitude of Scoat Fell is fully occupied by a very solid wall.

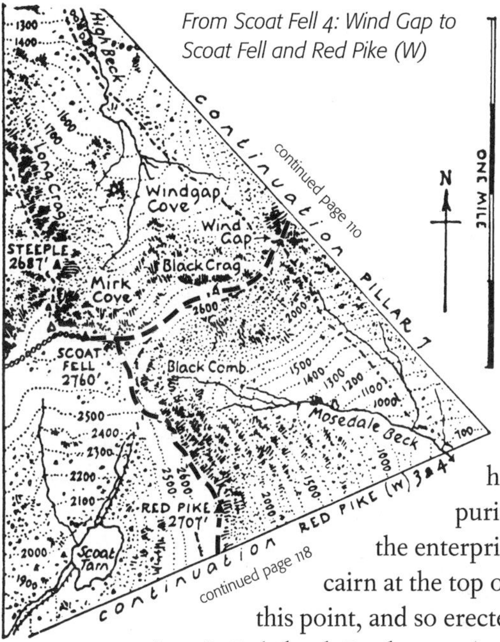

From Scoat Fell 4: Wind Gap to Scoat Fell and Red Pike (W)

continued page 110

continued page 118

Not to be thwarted, however, our purists have had the enterprise to build a cairn at the top of the wall at this point, and so erected an edifice unique in Lakeland. But less meticulous visitors will generally accept as the summit the prominent cairn on open ground near the angle of the wall, where the cliffs of Mirk Cove terminate in a gentle slope leading to the Steeple arête: this is a few feet lower.

The top of the fell, stony in places, is an easy parade but one is always conscious of the profound abyss of the northern coves close at hand and the gullies biting deeply into the edge of the plateau. Striking views are obtained by keeping along the rim of the cliffs and by following some of the headlands until they drop into space. Only Pillar of the nearer fells overtops Scoat Fell, and although it takes a big slice out of the distance there is enough left to see to occupy the attention on a clear day.

From the summit plateau of Scoat Fell, cross the wall at a gap and head down the slope towards the serrated escarpment of Red Pike. A path will be picked up but when it trends right keep straight on or the top cairn will be missed.

For a century, there has been confusion between this Red Pike and its namesake overlooking Buttermere (*see* page 82). Confusion is worse confounded by their proximity, the summits being only three miles apart. To make a distinction, it is more usual to refer to this peak as the Wasdale Red Pike.

*The summit of this **RED PIKE** has two large cairns widely spaced and the higher, at 2707 feet, is dramatically sited on the very brink of the Mosedale valley precipice and is so much on the edge of space that it cannot be walked round. It is a place to avoid in high wind. Yet the opposite western slope rises to the cairn in a gentle incline, carpeted with lovely turf. The transition in a matter of a few feet is a shock to the senses.*

The view is good only in parts. Scoat Fell and Pillar, nearby and higher, shut out the distance northwards and have little attraction. The Scafell range, seen full length and in true perspective, is the best feature. There is a striking aerial view of Black Comb.

Five hundred yards south is a larger cairn set amongst stones on an elevated plateau. This is the second summit, at 2629 feet, and is a typical mountain top in appearance and is often regarded as the real summit.

A summit feature that often escapes attention nowadays is an outcrop of rock that has been converted into a comfortable seat by the erection of a back rest and side arms of stones. This is The Chair, and was so well known in Victorian times that people spoke of climbing The Chair as today they speak of climbing Red Pike. It occupies a vantage point on the edge of the stony plateau of the south summit, overlooking Wastwater and is 120 yards south of the lower cairn. It is within twenty yards of the Dore Head track and prominently in view therefrom, but may be mistaken at a glance for a cairn. It has survived the storms of many years remarkably well, but it is not proof against vandals. Please respect it!

Now every step of the way back is downhill, which is not to say that all is plain sailing for the depression of Dore Head, quickly reached from Red Pike, occurs below the steep rocky slope of Yewbarrow.

The decent to Dore Head is just fine. The south summit will have been crossed, The Chair will have been found and sat upon, two rough rocky declivities will have been negotiated without much difficulty and a good speed maintained down the easy grass slopes. Steep scree and grass lead up to a barrier of rock (Stirrup Crag) that looks impassable.

Beyond and from it there descends into Mosedale a long strip of bare ground that formerly had a deep covering of small stones and was the best and fastest scree-run in the district. Now all has changed. Most of the stones have been scraped away by over-use, leaving the strip as an ugly scar, slippery and dangerous for anyone descending at speed.

Instead, descend the slope from Stirrup Crag for about 40 yards to the north (your left as you descend) of the original path and this will avoid the worst of the scree; great care should be

continued page 115

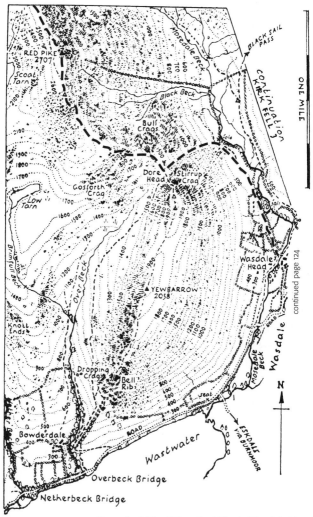

continued page 124

From Red Pike (W) 4: Red Pike to Wasdale Head

taken on this descent. About two-thirds of the way down, where the scree fans out in three or four fingers, it is possible to cross back onto the scree and descend the original path.

At the foot of the scree-run, a track swings to the right and comes down alongside Mosedale Beck, here fringed by trees and having a pleasant feature in the small waterfall of Ritson's Force. Then the walk ends happily with a stroll through fields and a crossing of the old packhorse bridge at Wasdale Head.

I think Wasdale Head must take pride of place amongst the valleys of Lakeland, not for scenic beauty but because of the sheer grandeur of its mountain setting. It is deeply inurned below steep and shaggy slopes, a patchwork of bright fields intersected by walls of massive width built of stones cleared from the pastures, an emerald strath circumscribed by rough fellsides overtopped by giants: the Scafells, Great Gable and Pillar. There is an inn and a few farmhouses and cottages catering for visitors. Wasdale Head is the best base of all for earnest fellwalkers and climbers.

I remember the inn when it was little changed from the days when that redoubtable dalesman, Will Ritson, was mine host a hundred years ago. On my first visit, it was still a haunt of climbers: boots and ropes cluttered the passages, drying jackets and breeches were draped over doors and chairs, all guests were seated for meals at a large wooden table and given no choice of food, in a room where the furniture showed signs of distress after being subject to demonstrations of climbing techniques; the talk was of climbing and little else, just as in Ritson's time. Ritson was a great character. Rough in speech, spirited in action, a practical joker of ingenuity, he was in no way subservient to the many distinguished men who regularly stayed at the inn and formed the fraternity of rock-climbers, nor was he abashed by their erudite knowledge. It used to be said at that time that Wasdale had the highest mountain, the deepest lake, the smallest church and the biggest liar in England. The biggest liar has gone but his ghost still lives there.

Today, alas, the inn has been brought into line with modern demands. Motorists have discovered Wasdale Head, and sandals are as likely to be seen there as heavy boots. But, seen from the heights around, the valley is as it always was: a place unique.

Standing outside the inn, it is easy for a red-blooded observer to appreciate the compelling effect of the surroundings on the adventurous Victorians who came here year after year. It was their exploits on the fells and crags, recorded for posterity, which put Wasdale Head firmly on the agenda of the generations of walkers and climbers who have followed in their footsteps and handholds.

Wasdale Head to Langdale

There is no other place with the magnetism of Wasdale Head. Great Gable towers magnificently over the valley, its tapering pyramid and girdle offering an irresistible challenge; Kirk Fell is a treadmill to heaven, and Lingmell directly opposite is a shield defending the Scafells behind. From the old packhorse bridge across Mosedale Beck at the rear of the inn, the high skyline of the Pillar range promises an excellent expedition, and Yewbarrow, soaring directly, not only protects the little community from westerly gales but is a fine viewpoint with surveillance over the whole valley.

If there is time, visit the church in the hamlet. Sad features of the tiny churchyard are the graves of climbers killed on the surrounding mountains. Look especially for the grave of Claud Frankland, who died in 1927 on Great Gable, after which mountain the headstone is roughly shaped and to which it forever looks.

This route to Scafell Pike has the single merit of shortness but lacks sweetness, every step being relentlessly uphill in harsh surroundings, but to its credit walkers get an impressive view of the mighty Scafell Crag on the way.

A footbridge over Lingmell Beck at Wasdale Head points

the way to a path rising across the Lingmell fellside where, upon turning a corner, the grim Scafell skyline bursts into view. The path fords Lingmell Gill, still not fully recovered from its battering during a severe storm half a century ago [the route is now fully paved], and mounts the tedious slope of Brown Tongue.

Interest quickens as the path arrives at the verges of an amphitheatre littered by boulders. This is Hollow Stones, deep-set below the cliffs of Pikes Crag on the left and the more imposing Scafell Crag on the right: a brutal scene, rather frightening on a first visit with a threat of disaster more apparent than real.

The path escapes from this inferno of rocks by turning left below Pikes Crag to the safety of the Lingmell col from which a well-blazed track, marked by many unnecessary cairns, spirals upwards without incident to the top of **SCAFELL PIKE**.

The difference between a hill and a mountain depends on *appearance*, not on *altitude* (whatever learned authorities may say to the contrary), and is thus arbitrary and a matter of personal opinion. Grass predominates on a hill, rock on a mountain. A hill is smooth, a mountain rough. In the case of Scafell Pike, opinions must agree that here is a mountain without doubt, and a mountain that is, moreover, every inch a mountain. Roughness and ruggedness are the necessary attributes, and the Pike has these in greater measure than other high ground in the country – which is just as it should be, for there is no higher ground than this.

It is remarkable that the highest mountain in England (3210 feet) should suffer a confusion of names. Scafell Pike was obviously given the family name of the parent mountain, Scafell, the original spelling of both being Scawfell.

The Ordnance Survey recognised three separate tops, including the then nameless peaks now known as Broad Crag and Ill Crag, as adjuncts of the highest pike, identifying them on their maps as The Pikes of Scawfell, later amending this to Scafell Pikes. Finally in the 1980s, they dropped the 's'. Broad Crag and Ill Crag are now commonly regarded as separate entities from Scafell Pike.

Scafell Pike is massive, shapeless and without even a touch of elegance. It has outgrown the head of the family but inherited none of its grandeur, the tremendous façade of Scafell Crag facing the Pike wearing a perpetual frown of displeasure and disappointment. The best the Pike can do to appease the old man and emulate his greatness is seen in Pikes Crag opposite, impressive in itself but untidy and a poor imitation. Admiration and attention are focused on Scafell Crag and, in such company, Pikes Crag is dismissed at a glance.

But superior altitude counts for much and the Pike is the magnet that attracts all active visitors to the district, giving them a sense of achievement: there is a unique satisfaction in standing on the very highest point in the country, an event usually commemorated by a personal celebration. Indeed, celebrations of all sorts from birthday parties and bonfire parties to reunions and memorial services have been held here. This is a very special place, and there is no other like it.

Scafell Pike is the supreme objective, the ultimate.

Scafell Pike is not an isolated mountain, sturdy support being given by adjacent heights that enjoy equal prominence in the landscape: indeed, in distant views it would be

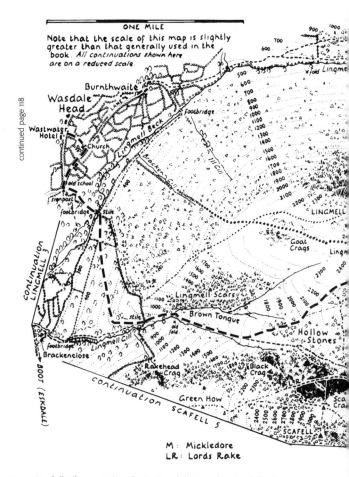

continued page 118

ONE MILE

Note that the scale of this map is slightly
greater than that generally used in the
book. All continuations shown here
are on a reduced scale.

M : Mickledore
LR : Lords Rake

*From Scafell Pike 7–8 (Book 4): Wasdale Head to Scafell Pike
and on to Esk Hause*

Sty Head

CABLE TRAVERSE

Spouthead Gill

Grainy Gill

Greta Gill

Piers Gill

Corridor Route

Stand Crag

Lambfoot Dub

Round How

tarns

Col

Broad Crag

Green Crag

Dropping Crag

SCAFELL PIKE 3210'

Broadcrag Tarn

Rough Crag

Broad Crags

Pen

Dow Crag

continuation

A: to BORROWDALE
B: to GREAT LANGDALE

continuation SEATHWAITE FELL 2

Sprinkling Tarn

to BORROWDALE

Ruddy Gill

continuation ALLEN CRAGS 3

GREAT END

Long Pike

Calf Cove

Esk Hause

III Crag

Calfcove Gill

Tongue

Cockly Pike

Little Narrowcove

continuation ESK PIKE 5

River Esk

N

C: to ESKDALE (via CAM SPOUT)

continued page 132

SCAFELL 6

125

difficult to identify the Pike with certainty had it not the advantage of a slight overtopping of its fellows. On one side only is there an uninterrupted fall to valley level, eastwards into upper Eskdale; elsewhere substantial buttresses, each a mountain in its own right, limit its domain. In the south there is a connection with Scafell at Mickledore; westwards Lingmell intervenes to cut off the descent into Wasdale, and in the north Broad Crag and Ill Crag crowd alongside to form the trinity of peaks. Despite its height, the roots of Scafell Pike are stunted by close neighbours.

Scafell Pike is the culminating point on a lofty range which, with four separate summits exceeding 3000 feet in height, is the most formidable mountain barrier in the Lake District and the roughest, much of it being a desert of stones. The range terminates abruptly at both extremities: Slight Side on Scafell overlooks Eskdale in the south and the well-named Great End falls away in cliffs facing Borrowdale in the north.

Scafell Pike was later a gift to the nation.

Tarns are noticeably absent on the arid, stony surface of the mountain, but there is one sheet of water below the summit to the south, Broadcrag Tarn, which is small and unattractive but, at 2725 feet, can at least boast the highest standing water in Lakeland. Crags are in evidence on all sides, and big areas of the upper slopes lie devastated by a covering of piled-up boulders, a result not of disintegration but of volcanic upheavals that laid waste to the mountain during its formation. The landscape is harsh, even savage, and has attracted to itself nothing of romance or historical legend. There is no sentiment about Scafell Pike.

The summit of Scafell Pike is also the summit of England, a distinction recognised in the proud days of the Empire by the erection on the highest point of a raised platform surmounted by steps and ringed by a substantial wall. This once handsome edifice is no longer in pristine condition, having been kicked out of shape by daily processions of visitors with no thought of the glories of Empire or respect for its monuments; from time to time efforts have been made to restore it. [The crumbling wall of the summit cairn has now been repaired.] Set in the outer north wall is a tablet commemorating the gift of the summit to the nation, and nearby is an obsolete triangulation column of the Ordnance Survey, a reminder of the days when mapmakers travelled on foot and not in aeroplanes.

The top of Scafell Pike is a barren desolation of stones of all shapes and sizes, difficult to negotiate, uncomfortable to walk upon and worn to a comparative smoothness only where paths have been trodden. There is no beauty here and only one rare patch of vegetation where exhausted bodies can recline. As befits its unique status, the top is rugged, sturdy and strong – just as it should be.

Inevitably, the summit is often crowded and noisy, not at all a place for rest and meditation, and visitors seeking quietness and privacy will find these blessings by a short stroll to the unfrequented south summit overlooking Eskdale, a kinder place, free from litter, where the silence of the mountains can be enjoyed in peace.

It is to be expected that the summit of Scafell Pike would have the most far-reaching panorama in the country, and so it proves. All the major heights in Lakeland are on display in a view crowded with detail and extending across the Irish Sea to the Isle of Man and, on rare occasions, to the mountains of Snowdonia in North Wales, the Mountains of Mourne in Ireland and the Galloway Hills in Scotland.

With many coastal features also in view, the identification of everything in sight is a task requiring more time than can normally be allotted to it. Most visitors are content to renew visual acquaintance with their Lakeland favourites from this superior elevation. The panorama is essentially of mountains; valleys and lakes are much less in evidence. It must be added that a complete all-round sighting is a bonus not often granted since the Pike is an avid collector of shrouds of mist and low clouds.

It is an exaggeration to describe walkers' routes across the top of Scafell Pike as paths because they make an uneasy pavement of angular boulders that are too unyielding ever to be trodden into subjection; nevertheless, the routes are quite distinct, the particular boulders selected for their feet by the pioneers having, in the past century or so, become so extensively scratched by bootnails that they now appear as white ribbons across the grey waste of stones. Thus there is no difficulty in following them, even in mist.

Most intimately attached is Broad Crag, 3054 feet. It is separated only by a narrow gap, the Broadcrag col, which carries the tourist path from Esk Hause and has recently acquired added significance by receiving a new path coming up from the Corridor Route.

Broad Crag is not commonly regarded as a separate fell, its summit being rarely visited although the path passes within a hundred yards and is little lower in elevation. The reason for this strange neglect is not clear from a study of the map but palpably obvious at the site: away from the trodden path, Broad Crag is a virgin jungle of boulders, piled one on top of another and settled at all angles, with a remarkable propensity for breaking legs – a desert of cruel rocks, hostile and defiant. Of the thousands of pilgrims who pass along the path every year, it is doubtful whether one even leaves the safety of the path to struggle in search of the summit. Broad Crag is an outcast, totally unloved except by foxes.

The western flank of Broad Crag is imposing. The top breaks away in a semi-circle of crags, below which is a shelf traversed by the Corridor Route and bounded lower down a steepening declivity by the great gash of Piers Gill. Only the proximity of the main Scafell Pike, overtopping the scene, robs Broad Crag of its rightful place as one of the finest of fells.

Ill Crag is the third of the Scafell Pikes, and the most shapely, appearing as a graceful peak when viewed from upper Eskdale where it dominates. Like Broad Crag, the summit lies off the path to Esk Hause but is more distant, although in this case too the shoulder of the fell is crossed at a height exceeding 3000 feet so that the summit is raised but little above it. The detour to the top is simple, only the final short rise being really rougher than the boulder-crossings on the path itself.

The route to Esk Hause is left when easier ground is reached above Calf Cove. Great End is then straight ahead, and gained up a gentle grass slope between boulders.

Great End terminates the Scafell range in the north and, at 2984 feet, is the only one of the five distinct summits denied a 3000-ft contour. It is not, however, at all the least worthy and, in some respects, is superior to the others.

GREAT END *thrusts boldly into space like a mighty headland, its height emphasised by a sudden collapse into cliffs, giving a commanding prominence when seen from other parts of the district. The summit, easily reached from the path above Esk Hause, has two handsome cairns, widely spaced, and the walk between them along the edge of the cliffs, punctuated by thrilling peeps down the three gullies that split the cliffs from top to bottom, is a pleasant stroll enhanced by an absence of crowds and litter.*

The justification for visiting the summit of Great End will be fully appreciated: a superb retrospective view of Borrowdale unfolds, extending from Sprinkling Tarn, seen as an inky blot a thousand feet below, to the fields of the mid-valley and Derwentwater backed by the Skiddaw group. In my opinion, the summit of Great End is a summit much to be preferred to that of Scafell Pike, not only for the Borrowdale view, which is superior to any seen from the Pike, but for its quietness and solitude and excitement.

From Great End, don't try a beeline because of acres of boulders. Rejoin the path from Scafell Pike to Esk Hause.

Sooner or later, every fellwalker finds himself for the first time at Esk Hause, the highest, best-known and most important of Lakeland foot-passes, and he will probably have read, or been told, that this is a place where it is easy to go astray. There should be no danger of this, however, even in bad conditions. Nevertheless, the lie of the land is curious (but not confusing). Esk Hause is a tilted grass plateau, high among the mountains. The unusual thing about it is that *two* passes have their summits on the plateau, two passes carrying entirely different routes. In fact, in general direction they are at right angles. If these routes crossed at the highest point of the plateau, there would be a simple cross-roads, but they do not: one is a hundred feet higher than the other and 300 yards distant.

The name Esk Hause is commonly but incorrectly applied to the lower of the passes, a much trodden route, but properly belongs to the higher and less favoured pass. What is almost always referred to as Esk Hause is not Esk Hause at all: the true Esk Hause is rarely so named except by the cartographers. The true Esk Hause (2490 feet) is the head of Eskdale, a shallow depression between Esk Pike and Great End – and the route of this walk.

*At the hause, continue ahead to a distinct track ascending interesting ground to the top of **ESK PIKE**. In mist, the path is easily missed, the natural tendency being to gravitate to the wall-shelter.*

Esk Pike is the central height in the semi-circle of fine peaks around the lonely head of upper Eskdale. In the splendid panorama of the Eskdale skyline the fell is the least prominent, not because it competes for attention with popular favourites such as the Scafells and Bowfell and the Crinkles but rather because its top is the furthest removed from the valley and appears dwarfed in relation to the others. Yet this is, in fact, a most attractive summit, deserving a separate ascent but invariably combined with a greater objective, Bowfell. Did it but stand alone, away from such enticing neighbours, Esk Pike would rank highly among the really worthwhile mountain climbs.

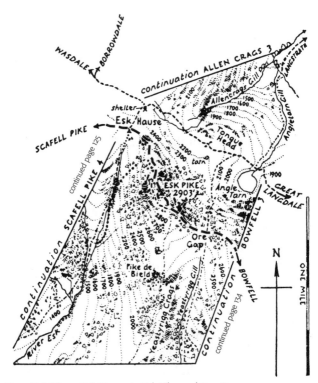

From Esk Pike 5: Esk House to Esk Pike and Ore Gap

The summit (2903 feet) is characterised by its colourful rocks which, unlike those of the other tops in this area of 'Borrowdale volcanics', are sharp and splintery, in predominantly brown or coppery hues with generous splashes of white and heavily stained with vivid patches of green lichen. These stones are profusely scattered and it is from a debris of flakes and fragments that the highest point, a craggy outcrop, emerges. In the lee of this small crag, which is cut away vertically to the north, is the most effective of all summit shelters.

The path across the top of the fell does not visit the outcrop, its obvious purpose being to link Esk Hause and Bowfell and not to lead its passengers to the summit of Esk Pike. Most walkers adhere to the path and by-pass the highest rocks [but walkers on this walk will surely visit the summit].

The excellent view is little inferior to that from the neighbouring Bowfell, and in some respects is even better, notably in the fine sight of the Scafells rising out of the depths of upper Eskdale, while the scene northwards is enhanced by the inclusion of Derwentwater which is not seen from the loftier Bowfell. There is an interesting viewpoint 60 yards north of the cairn and above a craggy buttress where upper Langstrath is well displayed beyond and below Tongue Head, the shelf carrying the path between Rossett Pass and Esk Hause.

A faint track skirts the north side of the next prominent outcrop along the top and then goes down to join the ridge-path, heading for Ore Gap. This is the narrow col between Esk Pike and Bowfell, and is identifiable when reached by the red subsoil of a vein of hematite that gives the place its name – which, occasionally and obviously wrongly, is spelt Ewer Gap. The crossing path is a route rarely undertaken between Eskdale and Borrowdale, the route over Esk Hause being preferred.

If the day is clear and time permits, a good alternative from Ore Gap is to bear left and over the top of Hanging Knotts to get views of Angle Tarn and Rossett Pass which will otherwise not be seen.

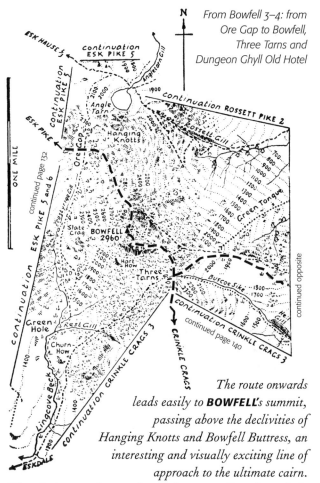

From Bowfell 3–4: from Ore Gap to Bowfell, Three Tarns and Dungeon Ghyll Old Hotel

N

continuation ESK PIKE 5

continuation ROSSETT PIKE 2

Angletarn Gill

ESK HAUSE 5

continuation ESK PIKE 5

ESK PIKE 5

Angle Tarn

Hanging Knotts

Rossett Gill

Ore Gap

continued page 132

continuation ESK PIKE 5 and 6

Green Tongue

Yeastyrigg Gill

Slate Crag

BOWFELL 2960'

Hart How

Three Tarns

Buscoe Sike

continued opposite

ONE MILE

continuation ESK PIKE 5 and 6

Green Hole

Rest Gill

Churn How

continuation CRINKLE CRAGS 3

continued page 140

CRINKLE CRAGS

continuation CRINKLE CRAGS 3

Lingcove Beck

ESKDALE

*The route onwards leads easily to **BOWFELL'S** summit, passing above the declivities of Hanging Knotts and Bowfell Buttress, an interesting and visually exciting line of approach to the ultimate cairn.*

The Ordnance Survey have always preferred on their maps to express the name of this noble mountain as two words, Bow Fell, and are correct in doing so if only in the interests of consistency since all other heights in the Lake District which have Fell as part of their names, such as Place Fell, Harter Fell, Lingmoor Fell, are invariably written and spoken as two separate words and never telescoped into one. Bowfell is the exception, possibly because the two words flow easily together in speech; the dalesfolk's local pronunciation being Bowfle. Since the turn of the century all writers have adopted the spelling of Bowfell.

A favourite of all fellwalkers, Bowfell is a mountain that commands attention

continued opposite

continued page 157

whenever it appears in a view. And more than attention, respect and admiration, too, for it has the rare characteristic of displaying a graceful outline and a sturdy shapeliness on all sides. The fell occupies a splendid position at the hub of three well-known valleys, Great Langdale, Langstrath and Eskdale, rising as a massive pyramid at the head of each. The higher the slopes rise, the rougher they become, finally rearing up steeply as a broken rib of rock around the peaked summit and stony top. These crags are of diverse and unusual form, natural curiosities that add an exceptional interest and help to identify Bowfell in the memory. Bowfell's unique secrets are locked away amongst its cliffs and crags but the key is available to those who are prepared to venture forth and make intimate acquaintance with the unique features waiting to be discovered.

Bowfell's top is a shattered pyramid, a great heap of stones and boulders and naked rock, a giant cairn in itself. The rugged summit(at 2960 feet) provides poor picking for the Bowfell sheep, who draw the line at mosses and lichens and look elsewhere for their mountain greenery, and reserves its best rewards for the walkers who climb the natural rocky stairway to its upper limit for here, spread before them for their delectation, is a glorious panorama which, moreover, may be surveyed and appreciated from positions of repose on the comfortable flat seats of stone (comfortable in the sense that everybody arriving here says how nice it is to sit down) with which the summit is liberally equipped. The leisurely contemplation of the scene will not be assailed by doubts as to whether the highest point has in fact been gained for rough slopes tumble away steeply on all sides.

The top pyramid stands on a sloping plinth which, to the east, extends beyond the base of the pyramid and forms a shelf or terrace where stones are less in evidence. It is from this shelf that Bowfell's main crags fall away, and from which, with care, they may be viewed; care is necessary because the boulders to be negotiated in carrying out this inspection are in a state of balance in places, and liable to keel over and trap a leg.

It is likely that the top will be populated by other walkers; if so, it is to be hoped that they are quietly enjoying the top and not being too noisily exultant about it. I like to have mountain summits all to myself. They are the loneliest of places and are best appreciated in silence. Human discords, loud conversations, shouting, raucous laughter and the modern evil of transistor radios are totally out of place. If such distractions occur on Bowfell's summit they must be endured, however, for the all-round view should not be hurriedly dismissed but studied at all points of the compass; this is a panorama that many consider to be the finest in Lakeland.

The sloping grass shelf, east of the actual summit, carries the only path across the top: it links Ore Gap with Three Tarns. A well-scratched track goes down from the cairn; it descends first in line with Three Tarns but is turned leftwards by the uncompromising rim of Bowfell Links.

Three Tarns (actually there are four) is/are set in a wide grassy depression.

NOTE FOR THIS EDITION: It is now necessary to descend to Great Langdale to end Day Nine. So instead of continuing forward to the Crinkle Crags, take a rough and steep path to the left, away from the tarns.

Although the grassy carpet has become frayed and worn by the passage of many boots, The Band is the easiest section of fell in the whole surround of Great Langdale, and is commonly used as a way down from Bowfell. The walking is easy although unexciting, interest being sustained by the impressive views of Pike o'Stickle and Pike o'Blisco across the enclosing valleys of Oxendale and Mickleden.

The path generally keeps to the Oxendale side of the ridge but occasionally crosses to the Mickleden side from where are fine views of the Langdale Pikes. The descent is down a long shoulder that springs from the level pastures of Stool End where the valley bottom is reached. Pass through the farmyard to reach the tarmac access lane.

A short way along the lane is the Old Dungeon Ghyll Hotel, the birthplace of rock-climbing in the valley with a wide selection of crags within convenient reach.

Those doing the Memorial Walk in its entirety will be able to make the Langdale Valley their base for the next two nights.

The Langdale Circuit

NOTE FOR THIS EDITION: Day Ten begins by retracing your steps from Langdale to the Three Tarns: see maps on pages 134–5.

From Dungeon Ghyll at the head of Great Langdale, a level strath is crossed on a farm road to Stool End, and the steep buttress immediately beyond is climbed on a distinct path suffering from popularity. This is a shoulder of Bowfell known as The Band, and the path rises steadily between the valleys of Mickleden and Oxendale. The ascent is tedious but relieved by some fine views on either side – the Langdale Pikes arrayed above Mickleden and Pike o'Blisco overlooking Oxendale. The serrated top of Crinkle Crags, ahead to the left, demands increasing attention as height is gained.

At the top of The Band, the terrain becomes rougher and steeper and the path then veers left into the depression of the Three Tarns. From the tarns, turn left onto a path to round Shelter Crags.

Walkers should pause on their onward route and, from the lower slopes of Shelter Crags, look back across the depression of Three Tarns to the Links of Bowfell below the summit of that mountain. These cliffs are unique in Lakeland: they are split by a dozen parallel gullies, alike in

continued page 134

continuation BOWFELL 3

Three Tarns

continuation ESK PIKE 6

Green Hole

Churn How

Esk Gill

Shelter Crags

CRINKLE CRAGS 2816

Long Top

Crinkle Gill

continuation Esk Pike 6

continuation Lingcove Beck

Adam-a-Cove

Great Cove

Gladstone Knott

ESKDALE

Swinsty Gill

Rayn Crag

Black Crag

x fold

Stonesty Pike

Stonesty Gill

Ram

Little Stand

continued page 147

Tarn

Tarn

Gaitkins

Red How

Cowcove Gill

continuation Mosedale Beck

continuation HARDKNOTT 4

2100
2000
1900
1800
1700
1600
1500
1400
1300
1200
1100
1000
900
800

ruin

x fold

River Duddon

ROAD

ONE MILE

N

HARDKNOTT PASS ←

Cockley Beck Bridge

*From Crinkle Crags 3: Three Tarns across
the Crinkle Crags*

pattern as though scraped out by a gigantic comb with the power of a bulldozer. The gullies are choked by boulders and spew out fans of scree.

Much of the following text has been re-written since AW's main descriptions of the Crinkle Crags ridge read from south to north, the opposite direction of this walk. Although it is usual to number the Crinkles from south to north, they have been numbered here north to south to tie in with the diagram of the ridge plan on page 143.

Rounding Shelter Crags, suddenly an assembly of Crinkles in close company is revealed directly ahead, Lakeland's best ridge-mile.

Bowfell's companion at the head of Great Langdale was given the name of Crinkle Crags by the dalesfolk of that valley because of the succession of abrupt undulations on its long summit ridge. Seen from a distance these seem minor and of little consequence but on closer acquaintance are found to be not merely crinkly but exceedingly rough with a covering of boulders that would be difficult to negotiate were it not for a stony track trodden by the boots of countless walkers. Even so, this track bypasses three of the five distinct summits to avoid unfriendly conditions underfoot although it visits the two other tops where the terrain is more amenable. It is difficult for a layman to understand why the mountain is littered by boulders in such unbroken profusion and even a trained geologist must have doubts. Normally accumulations of rocky debris are found at the base of cliffs from which they have fallen, but that is not the explanation here where they occupy the highest ground; it is inconceivable that there was once a super-structure of crags throughout the length of the ridge that has now disintegrated. No, this carpet of stones has lain undisturbed through the ages since the land was formed by violent eruptions of natural forces.

The presence of so extensive a field of boulders, however, should not be a deterrent to active walkers, the traverse of the ridge being amongst the grandest mountain walks in Lakeland and strenuous effort will be recompensed by superlative views. Timid walkers will be less happy and may find the mountain hostile but should attempt it: other mountains are climbed and forgotten but Crinkle Crags will always be remembered.

Topographically, Crinkle Crags is an immense barrier with rugged ramifications descending to Great Langdale, Eskdale and the Duddon Valley. The Langdale flank is buttressed by fearsome cliffs denying access to the ridge above, the Eskdale side is a steep and rocky labyrinth offering no invitations, and its roots in the Duddon Valley support a fellside of unremitting steepness. No Lakeland mountain has a more impressive surround of natural defences.

*The first **CRINKLE CRAG** reached in this southerly direction is Gunson Knott (2680 feet) and the path slants across the side of the mountain, bypassing its summit whose cairn is 20 yards east of the path with boulders on the top. The path bypasses the summit of the second Crinkle (2730 feet) too; here the cairn is on the edge of the crags 10 yards east of the path from where there is an excellent view of Langdale. The path is stony but not difficult; some writers have greatly exaggerated the dangers of the ridge. Nowhere is it anything but a pleasantly rough walk – except for the Bad Step; Bowfell and Scafell Pike are rougher.*

The next objective is the third Crinkle (2740 feet) which rises

RIDGE PLAN

for use when traversing the ridge from NORTH to SOUTH

● Read Upwards from the bottom

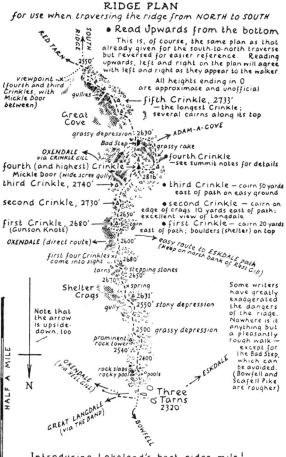

This is, of course, the same plan as that already given for the south-to-north traverse but reversed for easier reference. Reading upwards, left and right on the plan will agree with left and right as they appear to the walker.

All heights ending in 0 are approximate and unofficial

RED TARN

SOUTH RIDGE — 2550'

viewpoint x (fourth and third Crinkles, with Mickle Door between)

gullies

Great Cove

fifth Crinkle, 2733' — the longest Crinkle; several cairns along its top

grassy depression 2630'

ADAM-A-COVE

Bad Step

grassy rake

OXENDALE via CRINKLE GILL

fourth (and highest) Crinkle —

fourth Crinkle — see summit notes for details

Mickle Door (wide scree gully)

2810'

third Crinkle, 2740' —

● third Crinkle — cairn 50 yards east of path on easy ground

second Crinkle, 2730' —

● second Crinkle — cairn on edge of crags 10 yards east of path; excellent view of Langdale

2650'

first Crinkle 2680' (Gunson Knott) —

cairn

● first Crinkle — cairn 20 yards east of path; boulders (shelter) on top

OXENDALE (direct route) —

2600'

easy route to ESKDALE path (keep on north bank of Rest Gill)

first four Crinkles come into sight

2680'

tarns

stepping stones

2670' 2650'

Shelter Crags

x spring

2631'

Some writers have greatly exaggerated the dangers of the ridge. Nowhere is it anything but a pleasantly rough walk — except for the Bad Step, which can be avoided. (Bowfell and Scafell Pike are rougher)

gully

2550' stony depression

Note that the arrow is upside-down, too

N

2500' grassy depression

prominent rock tower

2540'

2400'

rock slabs rocky pool

pools

OXENDALE (via HELL GILL)

ESKDALE

Three Tarns 2320'

HALF A MILE

GREAT LANGDALE (via THE BAND)

BOWFELL

Introducing Lakeland's best ridge-mile!

like a pyramid from a desert of stones. Yet again, the path skirts its summit and a pathless scramble over boulders is necessary to reach its neat summit whose cairn is 50 yards from the path.

Bowfell, seen over the tops of the preceding two Crinkles, is seen but the gem is the prospect of Great Langdale in sharp contrast to the wilderness of stones all around.

Before reaching the fourth Crinkle, the wide scree gully of Mickle Door must be crossed. This is a pronounced gap in the ridge from which a vast screeshoot falls into Great Cove between confining cliffs.

The welcome spring on the summit (usually reliable after recent rain) is remarkable for its proximity to the top cairn on the fourth Crinkle (30 yards north-east, in the bend of the path); it is only 20 feet lower than the cairn, and has a very limited gathering ground. Find it by listening for it – it emerges as a tiny waterfall from beneath a boulder. This is not the highest spring in the district but it is the nearest to a high summit. The fourth Crinkle is the highest on the ridge, at 2816 feet.

There are few places on the summit ridge of Crinkle Crags where one can sit in comfortable relaxation or walk freely without having to measure every step forward. Rather unexpectedly, these simple pleasures are to be found on the highest summit of all. There, although perched on a rocky plinth with fearsome crags only a few yards away, there is no sense of danger. Long Top, as it is known because of a high lateral spur going off westwards, is bulky, not as delicately sculptured as the others in the family.

On the actual summit are two principal cairns separated by 40 yards of easy ground; that to the north, standing on a rock platform, is slightly the more elevated. The eastern face descends in precipices from the easy grass terraces above it; there are crags running down steeply from the south cairn also, but in other directions the top terrain is not difficult although everywhere rough.

The all-round view abounds in detail and you should not hurry from here. Bowfell has pride of place amongst a crowd of mountains in the northern arc and the Scafell range is seen to perfection above the gulf of Upper Eskdale. Of special distinction is the supremely beautiful view of the valleys of the Duddon and the Esk winding down to the sea; from no other summit are they so well seen.

Caution is needed on the descent southwards from the summit. A walker crossing the top from the north will naturally gravitate to the south cairn and start his descent there. A steep path goes down rock ledges to a slope of loose scree, which spills over the lip of a chockstone (two, really) bridging and blocking a little gully. Anyone descending at speed here is asking for a nasty fall. The impasse is usually avoided and the gully regained below the chockstone by an awkward descent of the rock wall to the left which deserves the name 'The Bad Step', for it is 10 feet high and as near vertical as makes no difference. Chicken-hearted walkers, muttering something about discretion being the better part of valour, will sneak away by following the author's footsteps around the left flank of the buttress forming the retaining wall of the gully where grassy ledges enable the foot of the gully to be reached without trouble; here they may sit and watch, with ill-concealed grins, the discomfiture of other tourists who may come along.

To avoid the Bad Step, proceed west from the main cairn for 140 yards to another on grass in a slight depression, whence a grassy rake on the left goes down, skirting completely the rocks of the Crinkle, to join the direct route at its base. At the foot is a grassy saddle which should now be crossed.

The fifth Crinkle (2733 feet) is out of character; it has a level top so progress is easy amongst scattered rocks and has a sensational view down into the deep abyss of Great Cove. After the splendid traverse of the final Crinkle, the nature of the surroundings changes completely.

*The large grassy plateau which follows after the summit of the fifth Crinkle stretches ahead; this may be crossed in a beeline but it is preferable, especially after rain, to keep to the Red Tarn path until a gentle slope, becoming craggy, leads easily to the attractive triple summit of **COLD PIKE**.*

The extensive southern slopes of Crinkle Crags decline gradually to an abrupt end on Wrynose Breast where they fall sharply to the infant River Duddon. Midway, their smooth passage is interrupted by the rocky ramparts of Cold Pike which cheekily apes its bigger neighbour by forming on a lesser scale a series of miniature crinkles, a jolly little set of knobs and pinnacles along a short summit ridge which is defended by a fringe of crags.

The summit of Cold Pike (2259 feet) is the best part of the fell. It consists of three rocky humps, each with a cairn and sprinkled with boulders, descending in altitude from north-west to south-east; the principal cairn stands on a pleasant rock platform. The view between north and east is very extensive, but on the west side is severely restricted by the lofty south ridge coming down from Crinkle Crags.

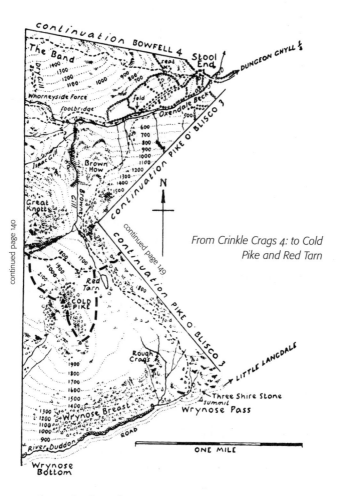

continuation BOWFELL 4

The Band

DRY Gill

1400
1300
1200
1100
1000
900
800
700

seat

Stool End

DUNGEON GHYLL ½

Whorneyside Force

footbridge

fold

Oxendale Beck

500

continuation PIKE O' BLISCO 3

Isaac Gill

Brown How

600
700
800
900
1000
1100
1200
1300
1400
1500

N

Great Knott

Browney Gill

continued page 140

From Crinkle Crags 4: to Cold Pike and Red Tarn

1500
1700
1800
1900
2000
2100

Red Tarn

COLD PIKE
2300

800

continued page 149

continuation PIKE O' BLISCO 3

1100

Rough Crags

LITTLE LANGDALE

1900
1800
1700
1600
1500
1400
1300
1200
1100
1000
900

Wrynose Breast

ROAD

River Duddon

Wrynose Bottom

Three Shire Stone
summit
Wrynose Pass

ONE MILE

Perhaps the best features are the two splendid lowland prospects, over Little Langdale to Windermere and the distant Pennines, and down the Duddon valley to the estuary and sea beyond. Red Tarn is rather an unattractive sheet of water but not without merit on a hot day. It is a walkers' crossroads since four paths converge near the outlet.

A cairned track leaves Red Tarn and, after about 500 feet of extra ups and downs, reaches the summit of **PIKE O'BLISCO** *(2304 feet).*

This fell rather suffers from the proximity of higher ones nearby, but quality counts for more than quantity, in mountains as in all else, and its abrupt and craggy top, much of it naked rock, would not disgrace an Alpine peak. The summit is a pleasant place and a colourful one, with pinky-grey rocks outcropping all around and interspersed by green mosses and dark heather. This is a splendid viewpoint, Bowfell and Crinkle Crags being especially well seen in their full majesty.

The summit was originally crowned by a tall and elegant cairn, a conspicuous and familiar landmark when viewed from Great Langdale. I always looked up at it when visiting that valley but there came an occasion in 1959 when it was missing from the scene. This was a shock: that fine column of stones, the work of a professional, had withstood the gales and storms for as long as I could recall. I went up to see what had happened and was dismayed to find the stones scattered on the ground. There was no doubt that the cairn had been deliberately thrown down. This was the first evidence I had that vandals and wreckers had emerged from their urban haunts and found their way up the fells. Regular fellwalkers are conservationists and never commit wilful damage on the mountains; they like them exactly as they are. I issued an appeal for volunteers to rebuild the cairn

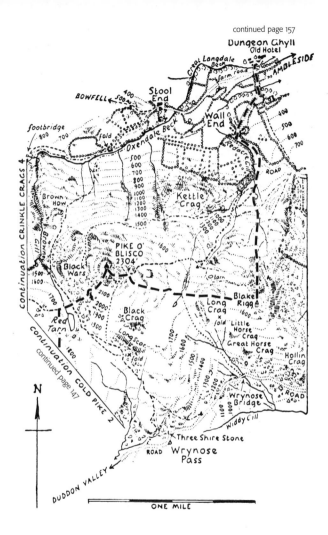

continued page 157

Dungeon Ghyll
Old Hotel

AMBLESIDE

BOWFELL

Stool
End

Great Langdale Beck

farm road

Wall
End

footbridge

Oxendale Beck

fold

ROAD

800 700

500
600
700
800
900
1000
1100
1200
1300
1400
1500

Kettle
Crag

Brown
How

PIKE O'
BLISCO
2304

600

Continuation Crinkle Crags 4

Black
Wars

1500
1600
1700

2100

Long
Crag

Blake
Rigg

1600

Red
Tarn

2000
1900
1500

Black
Crag

Long Scar

fold

o tarn

fold

Little
Horse
Crag

Great Horse
Crag

Hollin
Crag

continuation cold pike 2
continued page 147

N

500
1400

1700

1600

1800

1300
1200
1100

ROAD

Wrynose
Bridge

Widdy Gill

Three Shire Stone

ROAD

Wrynose
Pass

DUDDON VALLEY

ONE MILE

*From Pike o'Blisco 3: Red Tarn to Pike o'Blisco
and Great Langdale*

and, bless them, they did. To pull down a summit cairn is sacrilege. [There are now cairns on each of the two tops, one either side of the path.]

Shortly after leaving the summit of Pike o'Blisco, take a right fork on a path which leads over Long Crag to reach Blake Rigg. A sharp left turn here will rejoin the path which comes from Pike o'Blisco; it passes Kettle Crag on the left and drops down to Wall End. Here the little road joining Great and Little Langdale is reached for the final short walk to the Old Dungeon Ghyll Hotel.

A long look back at Bowfell will be a look not only of respect but probably even of affection born of an intimate acquaintance with this grand mountain. A final look back to the five Crinkles, aloof and seemingly unattainable, is the end of an enjoyable adventure and a memorable day.

Langdale to Ambleside (for Windermere)

Great Langdale shares with the Rothay valley and Borrow-dale the distinction of being one of the most tourist-populated valleys in Lakeland. But perhaps the word distinction, which implies pride of achievement, is not appropriate to the changed circumstances in these valleys since the turn of the century. When Nature completed her masterly landscape architecture ages ago and later the early dalesmen smoothed the rough places and furbished them with rich pastures and woodlands, then indeed there was distinction, rare and flawless, in the scenery thus created. Time was, within living memory, that a walker could wander all day in Langdale and enjoy undisturbed peace with the songs of birds and the murmur of waters as a musi-cal accompaniment; he would meet only a few others, and they of like mind, intent on quiet appreciation of the won-derful surroundings. We walked in fairyland. A solitary bus took us into the valley from Ambleside in the mornings and came back for us in the evening. Those were halcyon days, gone, never to return.

After the war, men's further contribution to this and other valleys has been to add blemishes where once there was perfection. The increasing invasion of motor cars and coaches, insensitively urged to visit the district by tourist boards and local authorities whose primary responsibility is to preserve the sanctity of their unique natural heritage, has led to the felling of trees and clearance of land to provide parking spaces; and sheep have been outlawed from their grazing grounds which are now used as camping and caravan sites. Inevitably commercial enterprises have sprung up like mushrooms to cater for the demands of noisy crowds of visitors, many of whom show little respect for the glories around them and prefer transistor radios to the muted sounds of a rural countryside. Local traffic is of course acceptable as part of the life of the community, but the mighty leviathans on wheels that choke the narrow roads are unwelcome and should be exiled. Langdale, which we old-timers knew and revered as a secret paradise, is becoming a free-for-all.

Yet these latterday disfigurements and irritations are merely pinpricks in the vast canvas the valley presents to its visitors. Great Langdale it is and great it will always be. The guardians of the valley are the Langdale Pikes, ranged like crouching lions eternally watching the happenings far below, often frowning at what they see but generally of benign disposition. They offer a welcome to those who come as on a pilgrimage to pay homage at the thrones of the gods and even enjoy a friendly tussle with the more active who climb up to pull the hairs on their chests. And they are part only of a majestic surround of peaks that cradle the valley in a loving embrace.

Once seen, never forgotten. Other places may slip from the memory but the distinctive profile of the Langdale

Pikes, once seen, leaves an indelible imprint on the mind. They are instantly recognisable not only by walkers and climbers but also by other visitors to the district who normally take little interest in identifying mountains and even less in ascending them. Whenever they appear in a view, they arrest attention. They are highly magnetic, constantly drawing the eyes and compelling the feet. To artists and photographers they are irresistible, yet their appeal comes not from grace or beauty, which they lack.

There are five distinct summits in the group, all within a mile in distance, yet not crowded together. Each has individual characteristics, being alike only in their very steep fall to the valley floor, their sides buttressed by crags and split by drainage gullies bringing streams down from the upper ramparts to join Great Langdale Beck and ultimately Windermere. These slopes soar two thousand feet in a lateral distance of less than half a mile and their ascent is a battle against gravity, a treadmill with the toil greatly relieved by scenic gems, imposing rock architecture and fascinating occurrences along the way, while the frequent necessary halts are regaled by lovely views of the green strath of the valley pastures below.

The five summits are, from the west: Pike o'Stickle, Loft Crag, Thorn Crag, Harrison Stickle and Pavey Ark, each of them having well-defined boundaries and claiming sovereignty over its own affairs, yet on nodding terms with its neighbours. Each too has natural features peculiar to itself and cannot be confused with the others. They are individuals, not quintuplets. All combine, however, to give walkers who attain the ridge a delightful tour of changing vistas and recurring surprises as their reward for the effort of getting there, all contributing to make the short journey, calling on each in turn, one of the finest miles in Lakeland. Nor is the passage from one to the other at all arduous, the hard work of the day being over when the ridge is reached. To be aloft up here with a few hours to spare is a joy known only to fellwalkers.

The five Pikes, although different in structure, do share in common the steepness and severity of the slopes descending to Great Langdale from their stark and angular skyline, leading to an expectation that the summit ridge will be found to be narrow and tenuous and succeeded immediately by similar steep declivities on the northern flank of the group. But this is not so. On a first visit, walkers who attain the ridge without consulting a map are astonished to discover that an extensive and uninteresting moorland continues north from the ridge at an elevation only little lower. From this side the Pikes are revealed as impostors, insignificant undulations along the edge of a dreary plateau. The contrast is absolute. The Pikes exhibit a bold front exclusively to Great Langdale. They are mountains with one side only. That one side, however, has more than enough to delight every fellwalker who sets foot on it. It is the Pikes' well-stocked shop window, full of good things. But the shop behind is empty.

The front view of the Langdale Pikes from the minor height of Side Pike across the valley of Great Langdale reveals in intimate detail the ruggedness of the southern aspect of the group with their distinctive summits and on the floor of the valley, disregarding threats of landslides or avalanches, is the little community of Dungeon Ghyll.

Ghyll is a fanciful version of *gill*, the Norse word for a mountain stream or a narrow ravine, adopted in the more romantic times when the writings of the Lake Poets brought the district into national prominence and gave a degree of sophistication to the places first visited by the early Victorian tourists. The new spelling of the name was applied mainly in the more accessible southern part of Lakeland, the most notable examples being Dungeon Ghyll and Stock Ghyll in Ambleside. Jenkinson's guide in the mid-nineteenth century would have none of it, but the hotels in Great Langdale followed suit and the new name is now firmly established.

Dungeon Ghyll is the principal stream coming down from the Langdale Pikes and its popular 60-ft waterfall, Dungeon Ghyll Force, is usually considered the highlight of the ascent.

If you start your day at the Old Dungeon Ghyll Hotel, it is possible to walk along the bottom of the fell to reach the path leading to Dungeon Ghyll Force, thus avoiding the road. If, however, you start from the New Dungeon Ghyll Hotel, take the much-used path leading to the Force.

Everybody halts here and many go no further. The Force is in an attractive setting in a deep gorge but is not easily seen when partly hidden by summer foliage on the trees lining the gorge. The path is directly alongside and soon turns left to continue the ascent, leaving the stream which comes down a rough defile on the right.

Above the Force, the path leads upwards to pass between Loft Crag on the left and Thorn Crag on the right. It is a very popular route and every turn and twist of the ingenious and circuitous path has been faithfully followed by many generations of walkers and climbers. It is full of interest until the plateau below Thorn Crag is reached; thereafter, less so.

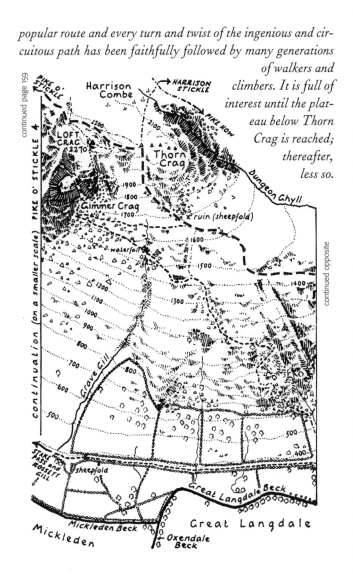

continued page 159

PIKE O' STICKLE

continuation (on a smaller scale)

PIKE O' STICKLE

Harrison Combe

→ HARRISON STICKLE

PIKE HOW

LOFT CRAG 2270

1200

2100

Thorn Crag

1900

1800

Gimmer Crag

1700

× ruin (sheepfold)

Dungeon Ghyll

1600

waterfall

1500

continued opposite

1400

1300

1200

1100

1000

900

800

Grave Gill

800

700

600

500

STAKE PASS and ROSSETT GILL

sheepfold

500

400

Mickleden Beck

Oxendale Beck

Great Langdale Beck

Great Langdale

Mickleden

Note that the scale
of this map is
larger than that
commonly used
in this book

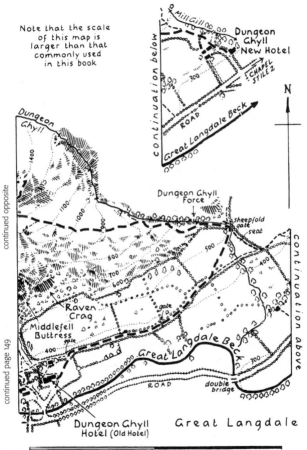

HALF A MILE

157

Thorn Crag, on the right of the path leading to Pike o'Stickle, is the least aggressive of the Langdale Pikes and hardly merits inclusion in their august company, its relative insignificance and absence of hazards leading to its selection as the easiest route by which the pedestrian path can reach the ridge.

This well-cairned path, which leads to the summit of Harrison Stickle, climbs the west slope of Thorn Crag and curves round the back. It is grass all the way.

On the left of the path is Loft Crag, a fine abrupt height of some character. It has the most formidable build-up of rocks in the Langdale Pikes group, Pavey Ark excepted; an upper fringe drops sharply to the huge near-vertical tower of Gimmer Crag, a top favourite among rock-climbers and often festooned with their ropes. Gimmer Crag is almost severed from the fellside by a deep cleft but admits no further weakness. Although it must rank after Pike o'Stickle and Harrison Stickle, Loft Crag is a worthy member of a fine trinity of peaks.

At the Thorn Crag col, leave the path which goes forward to the summit of Harrison Stickle, and take the left path for **PIKE O'STICKLE**.

It seems a fair conjecture that Pike o'Stickle's name derives from its close relationship with Harrison Stickle, being earlier regarded as a pike or peak of the parent mountain, and indeed it is the only one in the group sufficiently sharply pointed to deserve such recognition although all are now known collectively as the Langdale Pikes.

Pike o'Stickle is certainly the shapeliest of the group, the only one with pretensions to grace of outline and a pointed

continuation THUNACAR KNOTT 2

continued page 162

continued page 156

continuation (on a larger scale) LOFT CRAG 3

top. From all directions it has the appearance of a tapering dome, even from the north where the summit superstructure of 2323 feet is all that can be seen. Simplicity of design is another attribute that distinguishes the Pike from its fellows. A glance is enough for full appreciation: there are no ridges, no ramifications, no secret recesses. The Pike puts all its cards on the table: nothing is hidden from the sight of an observer. There is a feline smoothness and sleekness not usually associated with mountain structures but these are not weaknesses: on the contrary, the great unbroken sweep of the southern front, Stickle Breast, as it springs from the side valley of Mickleden is quite unrelenting through a height of nearly two thousand feet, narrowing as it rises in tiers of crags to the thimble-like top between two gullies defining its boundaries. Sleek it may be, but it is not to be stroked.

The summit is a perfect dome suggested by its appearance from a distance, being circular in plan and bell-shaped, with almost precipitous slopes rising up to it on all sides before finally tapering away gently to the highest point.

The top is a pleasant green sward of ample proportions, but exploration is severely restricted by the surrounding crags. Access to the cairn is gained by an easy scramble on the more broken northern slope, this being the only side 'open' to walkers.

The view is extensive, especially to the north, although it is interrupted in other directions by nearby higher ground. But the best thing to be seen is below the skyline: the head of Mickleden far beneath, with Bowfell a magnificent object as a background to the picture.

From the summit, retrace your steps for a short way, then take the path **HARRISON STICKLE** *(2403 feet).*

Harrison Stickle is the undisputed overlord of the Langdale Pikes. In height, bulk and in importance, it surpasses the others in the group; the kingpin, the boss, a cock amongst hens, not asking the lesser members of the family to bow and scrape for they too have their pride, but indisputably superior in every way. The top is a dark tower of rock, the object that most attracts the eyes of visitors coming up Great Langdale; indeed, seeming to timid observers to threaten the valley.

I once spent an autumn night on the slope of Harrison Stickle. I had walked up from the valley on a lovely evening and, after darkness had fallen, drizzling rain descended on the mountain. I had with me a khaki blanket, an Army reject, which served me well. In those days, I was rather addicted to spending nights out amongst the mountains. They were eerie vigils. The silence was absolute, the mountains were black silhouettes around me like crouching monsters.

I was always too apprehensive to sleep and passed the long hours of darkness with a cigarette every thirty minutes. At sunrise, the mountains changed quickly from black to grey to rosy pink and welcomed me to their company. After my first such experience, I quite lost my fear of mountains; they became friends. The reason for this eccentric pastime, apart from wanting to feel myself part of the scene, was that it gave me a dawn start on the tops and a full day's walking and exploration ahead of me.

On this occasion when the first light of day filtered through the murk, I went up to the top of Harrison Stickle and quite suddenly and unexpectedly emerged from the mist and saw before me the summit rocks, stark and clear under a cloudless sky. I walked across to the Langdale cairn and was transfixed by the most beautiful scene I have ever witnessed. I was standing on an island in the midst of a sea of cotton wool that extended to the far horizon. Across the valley a few other peaks pierced the mist, also like islands rising from the sea, sharply defined but sullen in the half-light of dawn. I waited for the sun to rise. Gradually I felt the warmth of the first rays; the summit rocks became diffused with a soft pink glow and within minutes were bathed in sunshine and casting long shadows. There was a profound stillness in the air; down below the mist, I could hear a cock crowing at one of the Langdale farms, but there was no other sound, not even the whisper of a breeze. Then slowly the mist receded from the shoulders of the distant peaks and settled over the valleys. Langdale was completely filled by a white mist that extended from Rossett Pike at the dalehead and curved like an unbroken glacier, following the

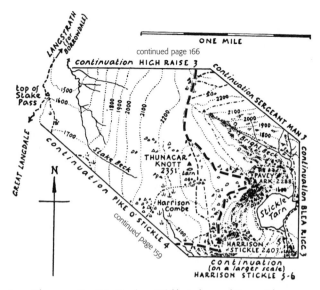

continued page 166

From Thunacar Knott 2: Harrison Stickle to beyond Pavey Ark

contours of the valley away into the distance over Elter-
water and above the length of Windermere to the sea, a
river of vapour, a mantle of unblemished purity. Alone I
saw it; there were people down there in their beds who
knew nothing of the glory of the morning. Still I waited.
Very slowly the mist began to break, patches of green
appeared, and within half an hour every vestige had dis-
sipated, and I could see the fields of Langdale far below as
on a map. The transformation was complete.

*The summit is an elevated ridge, 70 yards long and quite
narrow, falling away to crags at both ends. There are several
small cairns on the summit, and a large cairn to the south.*

The scanty covering of turf, scraped away by boots in

many places, reveals the underlying solid plinth of rock. The loftiness of the ridge and its commanding position endow a distinction to the summit that might be expected from the noble appearance in distant views.

Do not omit a visit to the south cairn which has a particularly good viewpoint. Apart from a view down to Great Langdale, Stickle Tarn is better seen from here and Blea Tarn comes into the picture as well.

Pavey Ark is seen in profile, its cliffs plunging down to Stickle Tarn in a series of buttresses broken by steep gullies. In the background, across the intermediate heights of Sergeant Man and Blea Rigg, is the long skyline of the Helvellyn range walked on Days Two and Three of this walk.

*Although not strictly a ridge route, the walk from Harrison Stickle to **PAVEY ARK** is a popular one. From the main cairn, descend the steep but easy rocks directly below to join a good path, much of it over bare rock, linking the two summits.*

Pavey Ark, 2288 feet high, is the grandest and most imposing cliff in the Langdale area, a colossus of rock of gigantic proportions, an awesome precipice that always staggers the senses no matter how often it is visited. In alliance with Stickle Tarn, which bathes the feet of this monstrous giant, the scene they present, while having nothing of beauty, has no equal in Lakeland: an awesome, almost brutal composition fashioned by nature and unchanged since the beginning of time. When this picture is suddenly revealed at the top of the usual path from the valley, the effect is electrifying.

Pavey Ark is set back from the other Pikes and does not

obtrude in the Langdale landscape as they do, nor has it their thrusting aggression. Of retiring disposition and remaining aloof, the Ark has a majesty and dignity the others lack; it is best appreciated when the day's visitors have departed and the great wall of rock is gripped in a deathly silence. Then the scene is overpowering.

The environs of the summit are delectable. Slabs and walls of beautifully grey rock, of rough texture not unlike the gabbro of Skye, rise from pleasant bilberry terraces, and some exploration is permissible here, with care, above the steepening precipices. Seated comfortably on the summit, one leg pointing to Loughrigg Fell and the other to Lingmoor Fell, the walker finds rewards for his toil, for between his feet is a gem of a view: that of Great Langdale's graceful curves, continued by the long sylvan upper reaches of Windermere, a view greatly enhanced by the steep plunge of the ground immediately beyond his boots.

From the summit of Pavey Ark, the path leads north-west to bypass the rather unattractive and little-visited fell of Thunacar Knott. The path from that fell to High Raise is then joined.

Leave the High Raise path not at the first track going off to the right at the depression (this goes only to a cluster of grey rocks, amongst which is a good windshelter), but further, at a scatter of boulders, where alternative tracks branch off to the right, both being continuous to the dome-shaped top of **SERGEANT MAN**. *This is strictly not a ridge walk, but a skirting of the valley containing Bright Beck.*

Sergeant Man is merely a rocky expression at the edge of the broad expanse forming the top of High Raise, but is so prominent an object and offers so compelling a challenge (in these respects being far superior to the summit of High Raise itself) that it is often given preference over the main fell as the target of a day's outing. Behind the abrupt peak, which rises steeply from the basin containing Stickle Tarn, is a hinterland of craggy outcrops and ravines that are rarely visited although yielding, in fact, more interest than the environs of the summit.

The stones around the summit cairn (2414 feet) have been scratched white by the nailed boots of visitors, testifying to the popularity of this summit. There is swampy ground on the top of the fell, and many small tarns. Sergeant Man is distinctive in having a stream within a furlong of the summit cairn, a point for specialists in mountain bivouacs to note.

The fine view is robbed of all-round excellence only by the tedious and extensive slopes of High Raise between west and north. It is a view of mountains almost exclusively, not of valleys. The most striking scene is that southwards, where Pavey Ark and Harrison Stickle rise starkly against a background formed by the Coniston Fells.

From Sergeant Man, follow a line of cairns north-west, left of the nearest tarn, and so join the old fence, which leave at another tarn around the corner for the big cairn half-left on **HIGH RAISE**.

It is usual to regard High Raise as Lakeland's most centrally situated fell. An area without definite boundaries cannot have a determinable centre and the 'most central fell' must remain a matter of individual attention. Nevertheless, High Raise occupies a magnificent position geographically, many valleys radiating from the wide upper

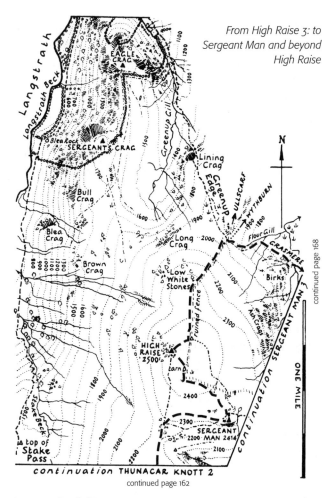

continued page 168

continued page 162

slopes. The fell's attractions, except as a viewpoint and an easy promenade, are limited, distinctivenatural features being absent from the rounded grassy slopes – remarkably so when one considers how full of character are the subsidiary summits of the main mass overlooking Great Langdale and Langstrath. Drainage is provided by these two valleys, Langstrath taking away most of the water, with the assistance of Greenup Gill and Wyth Burn in the north.

High Raise is often wrongly referred to as High White Stones. High Raise is the name of the fell, High White Stones the name of a small area of grey boulders which includes the summit (2500 feet). All else is grass, a vast sheepwalk in the form of a broad plateau little different from a valley pasture except there is much marshy ground.

The big cairn [now hollowed out to provide a double windshelter], and an adjacent survey column, stand at the top of the Langstrath slope, 150 yards west of a ruined fence: on the line of this fence, north-east, is a second cairn that features prominently in many views of the fell. [In fact, this is now a post on a rocky knoll.] Walking across the top is everywhere very easy.

From the summit of High Raise, continue in a northerly direction, passing Low White Stones, until Greenup Edge is reached; this is a gap on the ridge which joins High Raise and Ullscarf and crosses the path which links two of the most popular parts of Lakeland – Borrowdale and Grasmere. Although the Edge is wild, it is in daily use. [At the point where the crossing path is reached, walkers should turn right, here joining the route of Wainwright's Coast to Coast Walk until Grasmere is reached.] In thick weather, there is a danger of going astray by turning alongside the descending streams ahead under the impression that they will point the way to Grasmere, but the streams actually drain a valley that emerges at Wythburn. In

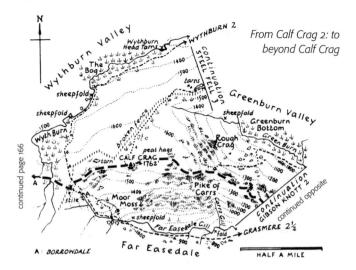

continued page 166

continued opposite

A : BORROWDALE

HALF A MILE

From Calf Crag 2: to beyond Calf Crag

clear conditions there should be no problem; the path contours around the head of this valley and ascends a slight rise to another pass formerly crossed by a wire fence of which only an iron stile still remains.

At this point, turn left along the line of the fence. After the first post is passed two paths go off to the right, one down the hill, the other along the slope. Take the latter path which leads eventually to the summit of **CALF CRAG**.

The familiar pyramid of Helm Crag, rising sharply from the green fields of Grasmere, is the terminus of a ridge that curves away westwards to culminate finally in the rocky crest of a lesser-known eminence, Calf Crag, and the route follows this ridge in reverse. The old county boundary traverses the broad top, but the highest point is wholly within [the old county of] Westmorland.

The highest point of Calf Crag (1762 feet), small and

rocky, is a pleasant place for a halt and quiet contemplation of the scenery. Sheep think so, too, and wearers of new clothes should not sink into repose here without first clearing away the profuse evidence of their occupation. Immediately below the cairn, on the south, is a wall of crag that constitutes a danger in mist.

*From the summit of Calf Crag, an enchanting track follows the ridge to the next objective, Gibson Knott. The path is a long succession of trivial ups and downs, and if it is adhered to too closely the cairn on **GIBSON KNOTT** could easily be missed – it stands on a rocky mound 30 yards to the left.*

At 1379 feet, Gibson Knott is the most elevated of the several sundry knobs and bumps that form the crest of the mile-long ridge linking Calf Crag and Helm Crag.

There is much rock in evidence along the serrated top and fringing steep flanks; in particular, a prominent

From Gibson Knott 2:
to beyond Gibson Knott

buttress, Horn Crag, adorned with juniper, rises from the bracken of the Easedale slope. The fellsides are 'dry', draining without forming regular watercourses.

The acute observer on the spot will probably question the earlier statement that Gibson Knott is the highest point on the ridge, for the next rise eastwards *seems* to be higher. Large-scale maps do not settle the doubt. *[The trigonometrical station mentioned by AW in his Pictorial Guide is no longer there; the path now passes between two rocky knolls each crowned by a small cairn.]*

*Re-join the path 30 yards south of the cairn on Gibson Knott and follow it east to the top of the next rise where it winds in and out and up and down in a charming manner before descending in heather to a grassy depression below **HELM CRAG**, a shapely pyramid beyond. The path goes steeply up to its exciting summit (1299 feet).*

Helm Crag may well be the best-known of all Lakeland fells, and possibly even the best-known hill in the country. Generations of passengers in cars and coaches have been tutored to recognise its appearance in the Grasmere landscape: it is the one feature of their Lakeland tour they hail at sight, and in unison, but the cry on their lips is not 'Helm Crag!' but 'The Lion and the Lamb!' – in a variety of dialects. The resemblance of the summit rocks to a lion is so striking that recognition, from several viewpoints, is instant; yet, oddly, the outline most like Leo is not the official 'Lion' at all: in fact, there are two lions, each with a lamb, and each guards one end of the summit ridge as though set there by architectural design.

The summit is altogether a rather weird and fantastic

continued page 169

From Helm Crag 3: Helm Crag
to Grasmere

Note that the scale
of this map is
larger than that
commonly used
in this book

continued
page 175

place, well worth not merely a visit
but a detailed and leisurely exploration. Indeed, the whole fell, although of
small extent, is unusually interesting; its very
appearance is challenging; its sides are steep, rough and
craggy; its top bristles; it *looks* irascible, like an unkempt
terrier in a company of foxhounds, for all around are loftier
and smoother fells, circling the pleasant vale of Grasmere
out of which Helm Crag rises so abruptly.

The summit ridge is 250 yards in length and is adorned at

each end by fangs of rock overtopping the fairly level path. Between these towers there have been others in ages past but all that remains of them now is a chaos of collapsed shoulders, choking a strange depression that extends the full length of the summit on the north-east side. The depression is bounded by a secondary ridge, and this in turn descends craggily to an even more strange depression, in appearance resembling a huge ditch cleft straight as a furrow across the breast of the fell for 300 yards; or, more romantically, a deep moat defending the turreted wall of the castle above. This surprising feature, which will not be seen unless searched for, will doubtless be readily explained by geologists (or antiquaries?): to the unlearned beholder it seems likely to be the result of some ancient natural convulsion that caused the sides of the fell to slip downwards a few yards before coming to rest. This ditch is also bounded on its far side by a parallel ridge or parapet (narrow, and an interesting walk) beyond which the fellside plunges down almost precipitously to the valley, falling in juniper-clad crags.

Care is needed when exploring the boulder-strewn depression on the summit, especially if the rocks are greasy. There are many good natural shelters here, and some dangerous clefts and fissures and holes, so well protected from the weather that summer flowers are to be found in bloom in their recesses as late as mid-winter.

Although a mere 1300 feet in height, the rocky crest of the summit is nevertheless the most distinguished of all Lakeland tops. Most prominent of its features is the sloping pinnacle, poised above a sheer drop, known as the Howitzer when seen from Dunmail Raise and as the Old Woman at the Organ from lower down the road.

Helm Crag has another distinction. It is the only Lakeland summit on which I have never stood. The top inch of the pinnacle is the highest point of the fell, and although I have been assured that this massive upthrust of naked rock can be scaled without much difficulty by anybody with a steady head, I have never ventured to climb up to its topmost inch. The situation is too airy for me. I do have a steady head but not as steady as all that. However, although I comfort myself with the consoling reflection that I am still alive and unscathed by injury, I wish I had done it, just once.

The Lion and the Lamb rocks are passed as the summit is left, the path then descending along the ridge to a little col, where it turns right, heading for Sour Milk Gill.

[Helm Crag was leased to the National Trust in 1961 by the 7th Earl of Lonsdale as part of the Lord Lonsdale Commons; the National Trust's surveyors decided to re-route the path to and from Grasmere in 1983 due to very heavy erosion. The new route off Helm Crag is clearly waymarked. The map on this page therefore contains amendments to that map which appears on page 3 of the Helm Crag chapter in the Pictorial Guide.]

An eighteenth-century writer described Grasmere as an unsuspected paradise. A paradise it still is, at least in appearance, but no longer unsuspected: indeed, it is a place internationally known and renowned, attracting visitors from all over the world. Many come to enjoy the scenery and to walk on the fells, and many more, admirers of the writings of William Wordsworth, are drawn by the poet's associations with the village and its environs, especially his home at Dove Cottage and the church. Visitors refer to this familiar structure simply as Grasmere Church; strictly it is the parish church of St Oswald. Of uncertain origin, but undoubtedly medieval, it is a building of unusual character, and the traditional venue of an annual Rush-bearing Festival. In the churchyard, a well-trodden path leads to the graves of William and Mary Wordsworth. Dove Cottage, where the poet lived with his sister Dorothy from 1799 to 1808, is now a museum for his effects.

Wordsworth's contribution to the prosperity of the area has been immense, but he would be dismayed by the extent to which the former charm of the village has been sacrificed to commercial interests. Once a sanctuary of peace and tranquillity, there is now a constant arrival of cars and coaches almost all the year round and the streets are overrun with crowds of visitors. Where there was quiet, there is noise. Only in the depths of winter can the village of Grasmere be visualised as it used to be.

But the environs are as delightful as ever they were. The River Rothay curves around the churchyard, its waters crystal clear, and lingers often, loth to leave an enchanting individuality for the anonymity of the lake. Yet it is the lake with its beautiful wooded shores and solitary island that is the jewel in Grasmere's crown, happy to indulge rowing boats on its placid surface and picnic parties on its shady beaches.

From the village, follow the Langdale road around the west side of the lake of Grasmere, leaving it by a gate on the left next to a cottage with distinctive chimneys. Keep to the right of the

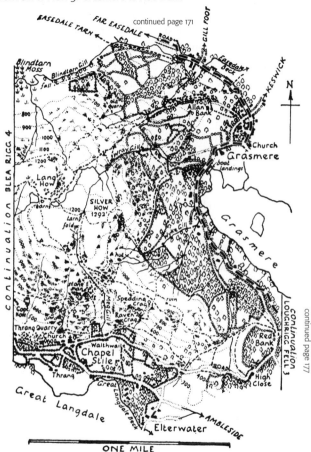

continued page 171

*National Trust sign and take a wide and pleasant path
through Deerbolts Wood, at the foot of Red Bank, which
emerges at the end of Loughrigg Terrace.*

Of the lesser heights of Lakeland, Loughrigg Fell is pre-eminent for it has delightful grassy paths, a series of surprises along the traverse of the summits, several charming vistas and magnificent views, fine contrasts of velvety turf, rich bracken and grey rock, a string of little tarns like pearls in a necklace, and a wealth of stately trees on the flanks. It has more paths to the square mile than any other fell, great or small, and amongst them is one that far exceeds in popularity any other in the district, one that all visitors know: Loughrigg Terrace which contours the slopes of Loughrigg Fell.

Here is seen a perfect composition, a masterpiece of nature, a beautiful and harmonious blending of lake and river, fields and fells, all arrayed in rich colours, with an overall prospect of the Vale of Grasmere and Dunmail Raise in the background. This is landscape gardening on a mammoth scale. And nowhere is there a car in sight.

There is yet another attraction in the form of a tremendous cave which may be visited if the walker keeps on the higher level when the choice is presented at the end of the Terrace. The cave, big enough to contain the entire population of Ambleside [or as the population was when AW wrote this chapter in Book Three in 1957], is a remarkable place although man-made and now disused.

The fellsides of this Memorial Walk are finally bade farewell at Pelter Bridge. From here, the A591 proceeds to Ambleside, now only a long mile away, but there is an opportunity to escape the busy main road. Do not cross Pelter Bridge but follow a quiet parallel road that copies the example of the River Rothay, keeping on its west bank through attractive surroundings.

The road can be followed to Waterhead, thus bypassing the

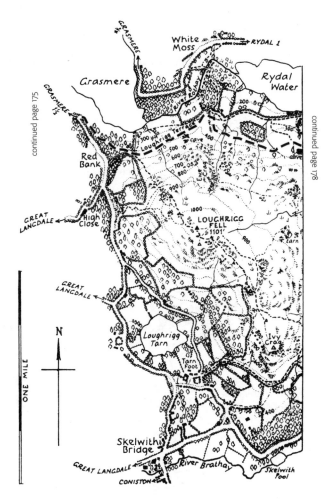

continued page 175

continued page 178

From Loughrigg Fell 3: Red Bank along
Loughrigg Terrace

busy centre of *Ambleside, where transport can be arranged for the final journey into Windermere. However the centre of Ambleside can still be visited: having passed the lane leading to Browhead Farm on the right, cross over the Rothay at Miller*

From Loughrigg Fell 4: Loughrigg Fell to Ambleside

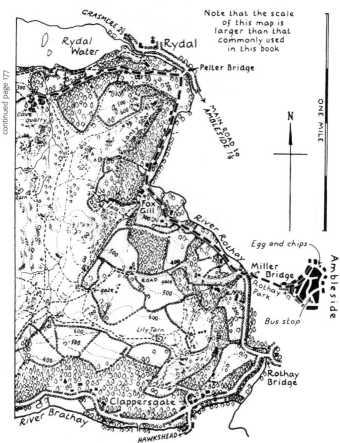

continued page 177

Bridge and take the path through Rothay Park to St Mary's Church near the centre of the town.

Ambleside is a Lakeland town that, by the good fortune of a favourable location, is known far beyond the district and even internationally. Apart from a huddle of picturesque old buildings on the hillside rising from the main street, the town is not in itself particularly attractive and has few items of architectural merit.

Its great appeal lies in the surrounding romantic landscape of valley and fell and woodland, in its fine position at the head of the largest lake in the country. On three sides the mountains rise abruptly and invitingly: friendly and colourful fells are reached, by much-trodden paths. Ambleside has been described as the hub of a wheel of beauty.

The crowds have driven the charm out of Ambleside. I am sorry to have to say this; as a regular Sunday caller here for many years after the war, I had an affection for the place. I discovered a small café off the main street where, after a long day on the fells, I was served with a large plate of egg and chips, and a huge pot of tea (the menu never changed) for half a crown. Almost always I was the only customer, which suited me because then I could study my map while eating. Afterwards I would make my way to the bus station for the last bus home. [Those walkers who need to return to Windermere, thus completing the round, should do the same.]

A. Wainwright's Itinerary for his Proposed Walking Tour in the Lake District

The route of AW's original Whitsuntide Walk was written down by him in 1931 and the pages later passed to one of his walking companions, Eric Maudsley. AW's daily itinerary gave the names of the fells, together with a running total of miles to be covered, the height to be climed and the time that should be spent on each stage. Thus, he expected, remarkably, to cover the 21½ miles and 6,700 feet of ascent designated for the second day in 11½ hours. Eric Maudsley said later, before the publication of the first edition of this walk, that Blencathra had to be omitted through lack of time. As has been written elsewhere, the route of this Memorial Walk does not differ from the original except the six-day programme has been split into eleven easier sections.

In the tables which follow, those fells which appear in the Pictorial Guide to the Lakeland Fells series are set in capitals and alongside each is given the Book number in that series and the Fell number within each book, the fells being ordered by altitude. The height of ascent between each successive fell is given (where relevant), together with the distance. At the end of each day, a total is given for the height climbed and the distance walked.

Itinerary	Book and Fell no.	Height of ascent (feet)	Distance (miles)
DAY ONE Windermere–Patterdale			
<u>Windermere</u>			
Orrest Head	O/F p. 26*	400	0.50
Garburn Pass		850	4.00
YOKE	2.14	850	1.75
ILL BELL	2.9	300	0.67
FROSWICK	2.12	285	0.67
THORNTHWAITE CRAG	2.4	480	1.00
HIGH STREET	2.1	250	1.25
THE KNOTT	2.10	200	1.25
ANGLETARN PIKES	2.26	250	2.50
<u>Patterdale</u>		0	1.75
Total of heights and distances		3865	15.34
The Outlying Fells of Lakeland			

Itinerary	Book and Fell no.	Height of ascent (feet)	Distance (miles)
DAY TWO Patterdale–St John's			
<u>Patterdale</u>			
Striding Edge		2230	4.25
HELVELLYN	1.1	470	1.00
Helvellyn Lower Man		60	0.50
WHITE SIDE	1.6	240	1.00
RAISE	1.4	250	0.75
Sticks Pass		0	0.50
<u>Stanah</u> (St John's in the Vale)		0	1.75
Total of heights and distances		3250	9.75

Itinerary	Book and Fell no.	Height of ascent (feet)	Distance (miles)
DAY THREE St John's–Scales			
<u>Stanah</u> (St John's in the Vale)			
Sticks Pass		1820	1.75
STYBARROW DODD	1.9	350	0.50
WATSON'S DODD	1.13	0	0.67
GREAT DODD	1.8	250	0.75
CLOUGH HEAD	1.18	300	2.00
Wallthwaite		0	4.25
<u>Scales</u>		300	0.75
Total of heights and distances		3020	10.67
DAY FOUR Scales–Keswick			
<u>Scales</u>			
Sharp Edge		1500	2.00
BLENCATHRA	5.2	750	0.75
Threlkeld		0	2.00
<u>Keswick</u>		0	3.00
Total of heights and distances		2250	7.75
DAY FIVE Keswick–Buttermere			
<u>Keswick</u>			
Portinscale		50	1.00
CATBELLS	6.24	1450	3.00
MAIDEN MOOR	6.15	720	1.50
EEL CRAGS/HIGH SPY	6.13	300	1.50

Itinerary	Book and Fell no.	Height of ascent (feet)	Distance (miles)
DALE HEAD	6.7	900	1.50
HINDSCARTH	6.9	250	1.25
ROBINSON	6.8	550	1.50
Newlands Hause		0	1.25
Buttermere		0	1.25
Total of heights and distances		4220	13.75

DAY SIX Buttermere Circuit

Buttermere			
Newlands Hause		1100	1.25
KNOTT RIGG	6.19	720	1.00
ARD CRAGS	6.17	200	1.00
SAIL	6.5	1000	1.00
EEL CRAG	6.2	320	0.40
GRASMOOR	6.1	450	1.25
WANDOPE	6.4	160	1.25
WHITELESS PIKE	6.12	110	0.88
Buttermere		0	1.75
Total of heights and distances		4060	9.78

DAY SEVEN Buttermere–Wasdale

Buttermere			
RED PIKE (B)	7.10	2150	1.75
HIGH STILE	7.6	350	0.75
HIGH CRAG	7.11	80	1.00

Itinerary	Book and Fell no.	Height of ascent (feet)	Distance (miles)
Scarth Gap Pass		100	1.00
HAYSTACKS	7.22	450	0.25
BRANDRETH	7.12	850	2.00
GREEN GABLE	7.9	450	1.00
Windy Gap		0	0.25
GREAT GABLE	7.1	500	0.25
Beck Head		0	0.60
Wasdale Head		0	3.00
Total of heights and distances		4930	11.85

DAY EIGHT Wasdale Head Circuit

Wasdale Head			
Beck Head		1788	3.00
KIRK FELL	7.7	600	1.25
Black Sail Pass		0	0.75
PILLAR	7.2	1150	1.75
Pillar Rock		0	0.25
PILLAR	7.2	500	0.25
Wind Gap		0	0.50
SCOAT FELL	7.3	300	0.75
RED PIKE (W)	7.4	210	0.75
Dore Head		0	0.75
Wasdale Head		0	1.75
Total of heights and distances		4548	11.75

Itinerary	Book and Fell no.	Height of ascent (feet)	Distance (miles)
DAY NINE Wasdale–Langdale			
Wasdale Head			
SCAFELL PIKE	4.1	3000	3.50
GREAT END	4.3	350	1.33
Esk Hause		0	0.50
ESK PIKE	4.5	425	0.75
Ore Gap		0	0.50
BOWFELL	4.4	400	0.50
Three Tarns		0	0.50
Great Langdale (Old Dungeon Ghyll Hotel)		0	2.60
Total of heights and distances		4175	10.18
DAY TEN Langdale Circuit			
Great Langdale (Old Dungeon Ghyll Hotel)			
Three Tarns		2050	2.60
CRINKLE CRAGS	4.6	600	1.00
COLD PIKE	4.19	300	1.50
PIKE O'BLISCO	4.18	700	1.25
Blake Rigg		100	0.50
Wall End		0	0.75
Great Langdale (Old Dungeon Ghyll Hotel)		0	0.75
Total of heights and distances		3750	8.35

Itinerary	Book and Fell no.	Height of ascent (feet)	Distance (miles)
DAY ELEVEN Langdale–Ambleside			
Great Langdale (Old Dungeon Ghyll Hotel)			
Dungeon Ghyll Force		230	0.60
PIKE O'STICKLE	3.6	1600	1.50
HARRISON STICKLE	3.3	350	0.50
PAVEY ARK	3.7	100	0.50
SERGEANT MAN	3.2	200	1.00
HIGH RAISE	3.1	140	0.50
Greenup Edge		0	0.50
CALF CRAG	3.15	150	1.00
GIBSON KNOTT	3.21	100	1.25
HELM CRAG	3.23	320	1.00
Grasmere		0	1.50
Loughrigg Terrace		300	1.50
Pelter Bridge		0	1.50
Ambleside		0	1.50
Bus to Windermere			
Total of heights and distances		3490	14.35

Index

Folios in **bold** refer to maps.

The Wainwright Memorial Walk Video

A 1¾-hour film of The Wainwright Memorial Walk is now available on VHS video. Spectacular aerial and summit photography is combined with Eric Robson's memories of A.Wainwright as he walks the 102 miles from Orrest Head to Grasmere. Along the way we meet many of AW's friends and followers – among them his widow, Betty, biographer Hunter Davies and three generations of walkers who've been inspired in the ways of the Lakeland hills by AW's classic fellwalking guides.

Also available are videos of the four award-winning BBC Television series that AW made with Eric Robson – Wainwright's Lakeland, Wainwright's Coast to Coast Walk, Wainwright's Highlands and Islands of Scotland, and Wainwright's North Country. The Wainwright Memorial Walk costs £12.99 plus £1.50 post and packing and the other Wainwright titles each cost £9.99 plus £1.50 post and packing. They are available from Striding Edge Ltd, Crag House Farm, Wasdale, Cumbria CA19 1DT. Credit card orders can be placed on Freephone 0800 027 25 27. Postage is free on orders of three or more videos.